SHIPWRECKS OFF OCEAN CITY

Drama on the high sea from Absecon to Avalon

by DAVID J. SEIBOLD
and CHARLES J. ADAMS III

SHIPWRECKS OFF OCEAN CITY
by David J. Seibold and Charles J. Adams III

For information, write to:
David J. Seibold
15 Hawthorne Drive,
Wyomissing Hills, Pa.

ISBN: 0-9610008-4-8

First Printing, June 1986

PRINTED IN THE UNITED STATES OF AMERICA

CONTENTS

ABOUT THE ARTIST

The original artwork scattered throughout this book is the art of Linda Perno Dotter, who created the pen-and-ink drawings especially for "Shipwrecks Off Ocean City."

Mrs. Dotter is a native of Long Branch, N.J. and today divides her time in Freehold and Barnegat Light, N.J., with her husband, Joseph, and four children.

She attended the Newark School of Fine and Industrial Arts, and has done numerous freelance art for various firms and organizations. Her work is also exhibited frequently in art shows in northern New Jersey.

FOREWORD

To the late twentieth-century visitor to Ocean City, this vibrant city by the sea is little more than an access point to the surf, a boardwalk full of wondrous activities, and a haven away from the rigors of inland life.

Indeed, the recorded history of Ocean City is, at best, sparse. Traceable as its origins are to 1879, this bustling resort on what was once called the island of Peck's Beach lacks much of the maritime lore its neighbors to the south and north along the New Jersey shore can claim.

Still, Ocean City's ocean horizon has been the scene of countless tales of bravery and tragedy on the sea.

There are no treacherous shoals, such as those at Barnegat Inlet, and there are no legends of golden bounty, such as along other stretches of sand along this coast.

There are, however, those undeniable and accessible wrecks such as the Sindia, the Azua, the Fall River, and others that have become favorite fishing and diving and, in the case of the Sindia, salvage sites.

As you read this book, and ponder its somewhat cumbersome subtitle, remind yourself of one vital fact.

The authors decided to incorporate the coastal wrecks of a long stretch of coastline for several reasons. All accounts herein are, as stated, "off the coast of Ocean City." Some will seem to stray far up or far down the coast from this focal point, however.

This had to be done. The dearth of recorded current events in Ocean City proper has resulted in most of the research being done in other, longer-established and larger locations such as Atlantic City and Cape May.

However, upon closer examination of several of the recorded shipwrecks which were, by Atlantic City accounts, "off the coast of Atlantic City," it was discovered that many were actually just as close to Ocean City.

Other factors that justify the wide range of this book are the peculiar curvature of the coastline from Absecon to Avalon, and the many inlets along the way. During the course of research, there were several accounts of wrecks and sea adventures in which it was obvious the witnesses or storytellers simply were confused by certain reference points on the shore.

Therefore, the authors have chosen to position Ocean City in the center of an irregular arc of approximately ten miles north and south, in which the wrecks in this volume have taken place.

The great majority of the shipwrecks in this book are of what the authors call the "blue-collar wreck" variety. That is, they often do not involve great loss of life or vast cargoes of riches. They do, however, typify the kind of story played out constantly off the coast of southern New Jersey.

GRAVEYARD OF THE SOUTH JERSEY SHORE

Modern navigational aids and weather prognostication have made the New Jersey coastline far safer than in any time in its history.

Still, it is very likely that news of a modern-day shipwreck off this shore could break at any time. Man and machine may join forces in an attempt to harness the unimaginable power of the sea, but the sea will always be the conquerer.

Ocean City, or more properly, "Peck's Beach," has been the scene of maritime tragedies since sailing vessels first visited the area centuries ago.

The earliest records of wrecks around Great Egg Harbor Inlet are incomplete and hazy. There are references to typical storybook treasure ships such as the "Dolphin," a three-deck Spanish galleon that sank near the Great Egg Bar in the late 1600s. With it, it is said, went its cargo of silver and gold.

Several merchant vessels, such as the "Betsey" and the "Delight" met their fates near Peck's Beach in the late 1700s, and as trade and shipping up and down the American coast increased in the early part of the nineteenth century, so did the number of shipwrecks off Ocean City.

The American Revolution was felt on the shores of Peck's Beach. The brig "Fame" was dispatched to this northern stretch of Cape May County to protect its residents from any possible British invasion.

William Treen of Egg Harbor, a veteran master of merchant and war ships, was in command, and the ship had already claimed several British ships in its tour of duty off the coast. On February 22, 1781, the Fame was at anchor in Great Egg Harbor Bay when a heavy gale brewed and capsized the ship in the bay.

On board were 28 crew members who frantically fought for their lives as the big ship foundered and fell to the whims of the wind.

Despite the bone-snapping cold of the water, four men leaped into the bay in an attempt to swim to the nearest land. Three of these men succeeded, making their way to the northern point of Peck's Beach. The fourth man drowned.

It wasn't until daylight the following morning that aid finally reached the Fame. Would-be rescuers found a horrible sight. A score of the 24 men who remained on board the capsized ship had died of exposure. The remaining four who saved themselves did so by walking briskly back and forth, stem to stern, on the side of the capsized Fame.

Some estimates claim that there are 2,000 or more vessels resting in eternal repose off New Jersey's coastline. The segment of that coast between Absecon and Corson's Inlets has had its share of those tragedies.

The earliest recorded (or, at least, remembered) 19th century shipwrecks include the "Belle Aire," of 1811, and the French brig, "Perseverance," in December, 1815.

The Perseverance was bound from Le Havre, France, to New York City, with a cargo of fine French linens, lace, and presumably a large cache of gold and silver.

The crew was looking forward to docking in America's legendary port city when one of those unpredictable nor'easters rushed in and began to wreak havoc with the big brig. The ship's captain decided to set every sail he could, and this proved to be a very unwise move. The forceful storm pushed the ship ever landward, until the deck watch shouted that there were breakers ahead. Valiantly, the helmsman tried to bring her about, but the storm had its way. The Perseverance tried desperately to live up to is own name, but failed miserably as it foundered in the shallow surf near Great Egg Inlet.

The waves pounded over the brig's decks and the 17 crew members fought for their lives. Some scrambled into the rigging and others to a lifeboat. Those who chose the latter wound up drowning as the storm upended the small boat and killed all aboard.

By daybreak, help had arrived from the shore. The storm persisted and nothing could be done to save those on board the Perseverance. As the ship settled into the sand, the remaining crewmen inched higher and higher in the shrouds, screaming for help. Some flashed money and jewelry to the rescue party in a grim inducement to continue trying to reach them. But like frozen birds, the survivors of the initial blow dropped from the yardarms to their deaths.

The captain perished when he made a mad dash into the water in an attempt to swim ashore, and a young girl, niece of one of the crewmen, was also caught up in the tragedy. Her body was the first to wash up on shore.

As the storm subsided, the shoreline along Peck's Beach (now Ocean City) was strewn with lace, bales of silk and satin, cashmere shawls, and piece of fine china.

Portions of the Perseverance's $400,000 cargo re-appeared on that same portion of beach when a storm stirred up the undersea grave of the Perseverance and once again spewed portions of china from the wreck onto the dry sand.

Storms play a major role in the continuing saga of shipwrecks along the south Jersey shore. A hurricane in 1821 took as its toll the British bark, "Syren," and throughout the mid-1800's, several more wrecks were recorded. In 1855, the schooner "James Page" and brig "Cardiff" were lost, and the "Rhine," which carried some 300 immigrants from Germany, beached at Ocean City, with all but one of the passengers surviving. A schooner named the "Sarah Hill" was listed among the missing on September 15, 1858.

Some historians made reference to a fruit-carrying bark named the "Dashaway," which was bound from Sicily to New York, but ran off course and came ashore at what is now Sea Isle City in 1860. Four years later, the freighter "Angela Brewer" was beached near 20th Street in present-day Ocean City.

The Brewer, heavily laden with a cargo of cotton and molasses to be shipped from New Orleans to Portland, Maine, was stranded in a frantic storm. All on board, including the captain's wife and two daughters, were saved.

The Great Egg Bar, one of the dozens of underwater mounds that rise and fall and change position from month to month, storm to storm, has claimed many vessels. In 1864, a steamer named the "Utah" struck the bar, and went down with its cargo of wine and china. The following year, the "Elizabeth," with 250 Irish immigrants, became another victim. All hands were saved.

On March 22, 1866, the ship "Amelia," was bound for New York from New Orleans with a cargo of flour when a nor'easter snuck up on her and pounded her hull into the bar. Six days later, the sandbar was struck by the schooner "Watchman," headed to Philadelphia from New York.

The schooners "Washington" and "Lady Ellen" fell prey to the shallows around Great Egg Inlet in 1871 and 1872, respectively, and on November 2, 1881, the brig "Zetland" ran off its course and was beached at Ocean City.

The Zetland was the victim of an unusual misfortune. During its voyage from Turks Island to Philadelphia, the captain took ill and died. His body was committed to the sea, and with his death came the eventual death of his ship.

Of the six crewmen, not a one understood even the most basic elements of navigation. The chronometer on board was not wound and the ship was helplessly lost. After running aground at Ocean City, the men were saved by the crew from the Peck's Beach Life-saving station.

With the need for effective coastal rescue services recognized by the federal government in 1871, the reporting and aiding of shipwreck victims entered a new age. Although formalized first in northern New Jersey, life-saving stations were positioned at fairly regular intervals along the beaches of south Jersey as well.

The life-saving stations at what is now Ocean City included the Longport station, at 23rd Street and Atlantic; Ocean City station, 4th and Atlantic; Peck's Beach, 36th and Central and Corson's Inlet, 58th and Central.

These stations, forerunners of present-day Coast Guard installations, were staffed by brave men whose tales of derring-do are legendary.

The life-savers of the shores around Great Egg Harbor Inlet were kept busy throughout the last decades of the 19th century. But even their skill and dedication couldn't save the eight men who died when a sudden storm capsized the coal-carrying "Deborah Diverty" in 1884.

In 1885, the brig "Maria" went down near the inlet in a March maelstrom. Around he same time, a schooner named the "Lottie Klotts" and her cargo of sugar cane and fruit was lost on the shoals.

Sometimes, the ships that ran afoul of the weather or were victims of their navigators' own mistakes did little to help the life-savers in their tasks.

Such was the case of the grounding of the Spanish brig "Panchito" on February 13, 1888. Although not technically a "shipwreck," as the vessel did not sink, the story of this shabby old ship and its motley crew is nonetheless fascinating.

The ship hit the Great Egg Harbor Inlet shoals in the dead of night, and immediately extinguished its lights. No distress signals were sent up, and for all intents and purposes, the ship and crew were content with their plight.

Contemporary reports indicated that the crew was barefoot, despite frigid temperatures, and all were wretched examples of humanity. The captain, said to be a rich Spaniard, had provided little or no substantive food, and the morale of the crew was as low as its collective intellect. The captain and second mate were both armed with a brace of revolvers, and appeared quite ready to use them should any of the rescuers displease them.

The rescuers came from the Peck's Beach Life-saving Station, and managed to take the 13 crewmen from the ship to safety on shore. The ship itself was virtually intact and seaworthy despite its grounding. After a week's work, the "Panchito" was floated off the bar and towed to Philadelphia, where it was abandoned.

It 1890, another schooner met its match on the Great Egg bar, and the "Louisa Robinson" added its name to the rolls of those ships lost near Ocean City.

The Longport and Ocean City life-savers responded on the morning of February 18, 1892 to the call for help from the schooner "J and H Scull." The ship was carrying a mixed cargo from Newborne, South Carolina to Atlantic City when the north bar of the Great Egg Inlet caught her. The crew was saved and most of the goods from her holds were salvaged. The ship, however, was a total loss.

An offshore storm on August 20, 1892 caused much attention on shore as word reached the growing settlement that several pleasure boats were in peril. The "Sallie" and the "Eliza," two yachts sailing off Ocean City, were swept by the storm, and the Eliza's owner and captain was killed.

Later that year, the coal-hauling "Marcia Lewis" became another victim of the bar, as did the schooner, "C.F. Young."

The Young had left Philadelphia with its load of coal bound for Portland, Maine, when the helmsman simply ventured too close to the shore on the moonless night of October 27, 1892. Once again, the Longport and Ocean City life-savers rushed to the bar, and it was initially believed that both crew and ship could be saved.

The salvage effort was far too difficult for what was available locally, so the Coast Wrecking Company was summoned. For three days they tried to pull the Young from the sand, but all efforts failed. The continual stress on the ship by the salvagers proved to be too much for the 214-ton three-master. The hull was split, and the sea poured in to seal the ship's fate. Everything of value was salvaged, but the Young was helplessly mired in the sand.

The year of 1894 marked the end of at least two more ships near Ocean City. One was the 2-masted schooner "Charles J. String," which was carrying fish to Milford, Delaware. She foundered on the Great Egg bar and sank on April 27.

On October 10, 1895, the captain and crew of the coal-carrier "Laura Reed" were saved after their ship went down in a vicious storm.

By the turn of the century, both communications and civilization at Peck's Beach had grown, and documentation of shipwrecks became more organized.

This is exemplified by the most famous, and certainly most documented wreck ever in Ocean City. That is, of course, the Sindia.

The story of this 1901 wreck is detailed elsewhere in this volume, but it should be noted that even the tale of the ill-fated Sindia is not without mysteries from the historically uncharted past.

Contemporary accounts indicate that the Sindia may have washed up not only on the glue-like sand of the 17th Street beach, but also on the bones of another wreck. This previous derelict gripped the hull of the Sindia, it is theorized, and held it fast. In "Heston's Annals," published in 1904, the author wrote:

> The submerged wreck which held the "Sindia" was believed to be the three-masted schooner, "S. Thorn," which went ashore about thirty-five years before and sank in the sand.
>
> The wreck of the bark "Lawrence," lost while on her way to New York from a Mediterranean port, on Ocean City's beach, was visible a short distance from the "Sindia."
>
> The hulk of the brig "Perseverance," which was lost about 1800 with a valuable cargo from a foreign port, was partially exposed at a place east by south of where the "Sindia" lay, with her hull immediately over and held by the wreck of the "Thorn."

In the yellowed pages of lost volumes and notes, there are many more shipwrecks noted. Some accounts include no dates whatsoever. The "Caroline Hill," the "Dart," the "Huron," and many more—all just names now. The "Henry Hobart," the "Ida Smith"—two more ships that have been lost on the beaches of Ocean City, and lost in time.

There has been death. Death such as the captain and a sailor aboard the "Sallie Clark," lost sometime in the late 1800s. And, there has been intrigue, such as the strange tales of how close the enemy really got to our shores in the two world wars of the 20th century.

In short, there is no way to compile a completely accurate

listing and history of exact dates, names and places of the shipwrecks at or near Ocean City.

This book merely attempts to pull together information from dozens of sources and provide for the reader some kind of informative, and hopefully entertaining reading.

THE RUM WRECK

Almost exactly one hundred years before Ocean City's beginning as a religious resort, a British ship called "Delight," with a crew of 29, ran aground on Peck's Beach just south of Great Egg Inlet.

The brig was on her way from Jamaica to New York with 180 barrels of rum and a load of sugar.

It was a stormy, foggy, spring day when the sixteen-gun ship gently struck on the Peck's Beach shoal.

The grounding came as a gentle shock as the captain and crew could hear and feel the rough scraping of the sand along the bottom of the ship.

On first examination of the bilge from the inside, there appeared to be minimal damage, so the captain ordered the crew to begin lightening the load by throwing items and cargo overboard with the hope the ship would ease off the bar and be able to continue her journey to New York.

The first to go overboard were four of the brig's sixteen cannons. Then, the captain ordered the barrels of rum overboard. Fourteen of the 180 barrels had been heaved overboard when the ship started to leak and break up from the pressures of the pounding surf banging into the grounded craft.

The grounding caused attention on the beach. While the crew labored to lighten the load, several local inhabitants of the area and the mainland came to help and maybe even pick up some cargo for themselves.

These were the days when looting and "wrecking" of ships were known to be a common practice. Stories carried all along the east coast about "mooncussers" and "wreckers" who would use all types of dastardly tricks to lure ships ashore. On a moonless night, these wreckers would walk a horse or a mule with a lighted lantern tied around its neck along the beach.

A ship following the coastline would see this light, think it was that of another ship following the coast closer to the shore, and maneuver closer. The victimized ship would find only shallow water and danger.

In both cases, the "wreckers" would hope for a grounding, and then loot the ship of its cargo, strip any useable lumber and sell the contents of the cargo inland. The lumber would be used by the beach bandits to improve their dwellings or for fire wood. Often these wreckers would travel in bands and would have a ship stripped well before authorities could get to the scene.

Perhaps some looting was conducted from the tragedy of the Delight on May 24, 1779, because several days later when the authorities did reach the scene, it was noted that only twelve guns, 80 barrels of rum and a small amount of sugar were found.

This remaining cargo, as well as the sails, cannon balls, gunpowder, rigging and hardware, was put up for auction sale to help recoup some of the losses due to the grounding.

There were 180 barrels of rum on the manifest. Fourteen barrels were thrown overboard, and 80 barrels were on the auction block. What happened to the remaining 86 barrels? Who says this area south of Great Egg Inlet was always "dry?!"

What probably happened was that most of the valuable cargo of fine Jamaican rum was looted from the ship, and found itself at many of the New Jersey, Delaware and eastern Pennsylvania taverns. Colonial days black marketing was a thriving and profitable business.

In the history of Ocean City, written by Harold Lee, the author noted that one of the four 9-pound cannons thrown overboard to lighten the ship was recovered in 1820 by Uriah Smith and "taken to the mainland below Palermo, where it was placed at the entrance to the lane that became known as Cannon Road."

Mr. Lee further writes that in 1906, it was returned to the beach where Smith found it, and became a monument on the Camp Ground.

The historic cannon, probably the last surviving relic from the wreck of the brig "Delight," simply disappeared in the summer of 1966, and hasn't been seen since.

A DARING RESCUE

As the title of this chapter indicates, this is the tale of a rescue. But it is also a story about yet another sailor driven to his untimely death off the treacherous South Jersey coastline.

All was going well for the two-master "James C. Fisher" as it sailed out of Smyrna Creek, Delaware on New Year's Eve, 1852.

Headed with a belly full of grain bound for New York City, the schooner made Cape May early on the first day of 1853 and was greeted by headwinds as she assumed a northerly course.

Captain John T. Anderson was young and strong, and the Fisher was a seaworthy craft. Its crew consisted of Charles Postles of Milford, Delaware; Peter Keen, of Main; Mitchell Hopkins of Philadelphia; Thomas Morris of Smyrna, Delaware; and James Turner, of Milford, Delaware, the ship's cook.

The first mate was Garret L. Hynson, a 23-year old who had just shipped out to sea two years prior to the incident that would forever change his life.

Hynson was an interesting character. His father was a well-known writer in Delaware and a Baptist minister. Young Garret left Rev. Mathew and Anna Hynson's Milford area farm for adventure on the high seas, and found perhaps the ultimate adventure aboard the James C. Fisher.

Apparently, some of Garret's father's writing skills and desire were passed on to the younger man, because it is his vivid account that provides the information about the wreck, death and rescue of the Fisher and her men.

As the ship reached Great Egg Harbor, on January 2, 1853, the breeze began to become more unpredictable. A storm, a beastly Nor'easter, was brewing ahead.

"The captain decided to turn back and run in the capes again to get out of the storm," wrote Garret Hynson, "but after sundown the wind reached the velocity of a gale and was accompanied by rain. It was not long before a portion of the rigging was blown away."

"The captain tried to sight Cape May Light, but got too close in and the schooner suddenly struck her bottom. The sea swept the decks with terrific force, washing everything away. The men then took to the rigging."

Hynson continued to detail the grounding, noting that the captain's decision to "let go the big anchor" had proven to be disastrous.

"It was as dark as Egypt and the roar of the sea, the wind and the rain was deafening," he said. "At last the bottom of the schooner was crushed in and she bilged and settled down from the wind, making her a bulwark to the sea. She was no longer buoyant."

The mate said the men decided to leave the rigging, strip the cabin and escape with whatever they could carry.

"It was 2:20 o'clock on Tuesday morning when I left the cabin for I distinctly remember looking at the marine clock," wrote Hynson. The vessel again settled down and the men, all pretty well exhausted, were praying for daylight and wondering how they were to be rescued. They did not know where they were and to add to their misery, snow began to fall in great flakes before daylight."

The beach was about thirty yards away. It would have been a dangerous feat to swim to shore, but Hynson knew it was the only way to find salvation.

The current and undertow were strong. Just a few minutes in the frigid water could kill a man. But Hynson was determined. At about 8:30 in the morning, he leaped overboard dressed in a heavy overcoat, cap and boots.

He swam through the icy surf, but made little headway as the waves pushed him and pulled him at will.

His recollection was vivid: "Tired out and discouraged, I thought I must surely drown, but struck out again. At last, my toes touched bottom but a heavy sea tripped me and I floundered in the breakers. Another effort and I found I could stand, the water reaching to my waist only.

"When the crew in the rigging saw that I was ashore, they sent up a feeble cheer. I thought that I must surely find someone and started north up the beach. I never saw it snow harder. I wandered up and down on the beach all day, passing the ship once or twice in my search of some habitation."

Hynson spent a full day wandering the beach, but discovered no signs of human life. His body numbed by the January snow storm, and darkness setting in, he decided to bed down for the night in a thicket, and resume his search in the morning, if he indeed lived through the night.

The sun rose on Wednesday, January 4, 1853, and Hynson found that he was at the end of a beach, at an inlet. Across the inlet, there were houses visible and smoke was billowing from the chimneys.

"I threw my hat in the air to attract attention if possible, but no one saw me," he recalled. "Discouraged and almost dead, I returned to the vessel. The men were still in the rigging, with the exception of the cook. The captain was dead. The men made a faint cry when they saw me but they had been exposed so long they had little strength.

Finally, at about noontime, three strangers showed up on the beach. Two of the three men refused to help rescue Hynson's shipmates, saying the rough seas would make such an attempt impossible.

But one man, identified as James Richardson, said he would set out in his yawl and do his best to bring the men to safety.

Hynson continued: "He and I started out and succeeded in reaching the schooner safely.

"The men were stiff and unable to help themselves, but we helped one in at a time out of the rigging with great difficulty. Richardson took them ashore one at a time, where they were cared for by Richardson's father and another man. The body of the captain, who had been lashed in the cabin, was towed ashore, the dead weight being too much for the yawl."

It took months, even years, for the frozen hands and feet of the crewmen to return to normal. Hynson said it took a year before he was able to put shoes on once again and seven years before his feet completely healed. "When my boots were cut off at Cape May Court House," he said, "the doctor thought he would have to take my toes off. The ice was solid between my toes."

It should be remembered that this was well before the formation of the coastal Life-Saving Service. Hynson (so persuasive that in 1888 he was elected as a state legislator in Delaware) and his story of one man's determination and another's bravery, pressed the issue.

There were rough-hewn cabins and tents manned from time to time at spotty locations up and down the coast, but there was no formalized coastal rescue service. The wreck of the Fisher, the suffering of her crew and the death of her captain may very well have hastened the formation and establishment of the federal Life-Saving Service in 1871.

THE SINDIA

If you visit Ocean City but once, the chances are that you will go away with a fair knowledge of the ill-fated bark named the Sindia.

It is, arguably, the most famous of all the shipwrecks along the New Jersey shore. Its bones, rotted and eaten away by time and tide, have taken up permanent residence in the sands of the 17th Street beach and are occasionally visible at low tide.

The most profound reminder of this wreck is very visible. It pokes out of the sand and surf as a monument to the giant vessel that, through a strange and still mysterious twist of misfortune and malfeasance, became stranded on the beach during a strong December gale in 1901.

The scant remains of the Sindia that can be seen on the beach may not be all that is left of the freighter. Treasure-seeking divers truly believe that the ship's corpse, buried deeply in the sand, may hold within it a trove worth several million dollars.

Salvage attempts in recent years have borne no fruit. Still, the most recent plans call for digging deep into the sand and diving into the murky mess in hopes of retrieving whatever could still be down there.

This booty might include thousands of pieces of bronze. It could include bits of china (exploration into the sand in the early 1980s recovered four or five cups and saucers), and it could include nothing of any real value at all.

Still, man's insatiable curiosity and quest for adventure will doubtlessly result in more divers digging deeper—literally "mining" the sand—for whatever can be found, trinket or treasure.

One firm has instituted legal and financial arrangements

with state and federal authorities to seek the claim to salvage rights of the Sindia. They are hopeful that any items brought up could be sold or exhibited, and the usual book-film deal could be struck. Such an arrangement could reap economic gain for the company, and under state laws, one-third of the value of whatever is plucked from the wreck would be retained by the salvagers. The state of New Jersey would receive the rest.

The proposed salvage operation has run into several snags. The state requires certain assurances, the city of Ocean City wants a $50,000 bond up front, neighbors with possible riparian rights have put up a fuss, and the shifting sands themselves have proven very reluctant to give up their bounty.

Therein lies one of the biggest problems the would-be salvagers might face. There is a very good chance that there is virtually nothing of value within the twisted and rusted metal of what was once a 329-foot long iron-hulled veteran of the East Indian trade routes.

Some say that only a minute portion of the bronze and porcelain and china was taken off the ship before it was sucked into the sand. Others say whatever was of real value was taken off the ship almost immediately after the beaching and thousands upon thousands of other artifacts were rifled by souvenir hunters and outright thieves.

The tales of the pillaging of the Sindia after it drifted ashore on that cold December day are some of the more colorful in the annals of Ocean City.

There is evidence that a great amount of the cargo was offloaded by a New York-based wrecking company. Later, divers and salvagers took what was left. Countless Ocean City homes have prized pieces of the Sindia's cargo, handed down from one generation to the next. The Ocean City Historical Museum has a dazzling collection of items from the ship in its "Sindia Room," in addition to a fine array of photographs and documents chronicling the life, loss and legend of the great vessel.

Oh yes—the LEGEND of the Sindia. Lest we not forget the greatest mystery of all that surround this storied ship.

It is said that aboard the Sindia at the time of its grounding at Ocean City was the two-ton statue of Buddha, plundered from an Oriental temple and secreted in the holds of the British ship just before it left for what was to be its final, fatal voyage.

The Buddha, if there was one, was made of stone or perhaps bronze. And with it, legend has it, came a curse.

This curse is blamed for the wreck of the Sindia, the bizarre events that followed, and the hulk's reluctance to give up its contents to modern-day salvagers.

It may be just a fanciful story that somehow was attached to the Sindia, but even the divers who most recently attempted to dig into the sands and to the Sindia's mysteries acknowledge that an unseen force seems to be toying with their mission.

As one peruses the marvelous Sindia Room of the Ocean City Historical Museum, it is easy to conjure up the many unanswered questions about the wreck. Yellowed and crinkled photographs record the grounding, and the steady breaking up of the 3,000 ton vessel that stretches across the beach longer than the length of a football field.

Examples of the prizes taken from the ship are spectacular now, but were considered—for the most part—tawdry carnival curios in the early 1900s.

A visit to the museum, coupled with a walk to the Sindia's sad tomb can prove to tie together two ends of a haunting nautical story.

The very name of the vessel is interesting. "Sindia" was the family name of a dynasty in central India in the late 18th and early 19th century. There is no record as to the application of the name to the ship.

The ship was built in the fabled Harland and Wolff yards in Belfast in 1887. She sailed out of Liverpool and logged nearly a quarter of a million miles at sea before her destiny at Ocean City.

Considered the fastest ship of her kind in her prime, the Sindia left for a trip halfway across the globe and back shortly after being purchased from the Brocklebank Shipping firm by the Anglo-American Oil Company for $200,000 in 1900.

The ship's first assignment was to transport a bellyful of oil from New York to Shanghai, China. After this was done, the Sindia left for Kobe, Japan, to load a mixed cargo of matting, screens, wax, camphor oil, linseed, manganese and the more than 3,300 boxes of "curios."

The ship's manifest also listed much smaller quantities of bamboo and sassafras oil, but there is no mention of bronze or comparably worthwhile items.

On July 8, 1901, the Sindia sailed out of Kobe, headed for Cape Horn and then northward to New York. She was a rugged vessel, designed both for speed and endurance. Even in death on the beach of Ocean City, the Sindia's four raked masts and sleek, servicable hull retained their majesty.

She was captained by a well-respected master, Captain Allen McKenzie. He had no idea that his career, and perhaps his entire life, would be inexorably altered by the chain of events off the coast of New Jersey a half-year after leaving Japan. But then again, perhaps he believed in the "curse" of the Buddha (if there was one) and knew somehow that the voyage, the ship, and his proud record at sea, were doomed.

The journey of 10,000 miles from Kobe to New York started, continued and almost ended without incident. The dynamic Scotsman captained his vessel around the Horn and prepared for an unremarkable final leg home.

The broad Pacific, dangerous Cape Horn, the rough and tumble South Atlantic and the equatorial waters were kind to the Sindia. But the unpredictable seas and weather off South Jersey proved to be the Sindia's undoing.

The crew of 33 was probably thinking of a Christmas with family and friends. There were stories about some rather reckless merry-making going on the night of December 14, a couple of days before the expected arrival in New York. Some accounts hold that the majority of the crew was, in briefest terms, quite drunk that night. It was reputed (and later refuted) that this overuse of grog contributed directly to the foundering of the big ship.

In 1964, the last surviving member of the Sindia crew, David Jackson Sr., was confronted with the popular rumor that the crewmen were intoxicated that night. He shot back to the interviewer, affirming in no uncertain terms that, in his words, "there wasn't enough grog aboard to get a baby drunk!"

This claim notwithstanding, something went very wrong on the night of December 14, 1901. The Sindia had just passed

Cape May when an icy storm punched the Sindia like a giant fist. It drove the ship toward the shore relentlessly. By midnight, the storm was at its most violent peak. Through the wee small hours of December 15, the storm played with the Sindia as if it was a toy boat.

It is at this point that the drama and the questions of the conduct of captain and crew begin to expand. As soundings were taken at about 1 a.m., the captain was certain that the ship was on course and in safe waters.

As the storm intensified, the Sindia's seagoing integrity faltered. For whatever reasons, the ship drifted ever closer to the shoreline, seemingly giving up the fight to stay in deeper water.

The first evidence that the Sindia was in real trouble came at 2:30 a.m. when the first distress signal rockets were sent aloft. It was clear that the ship, now with bow pointing due west, would be trapped in the swirling surf.

At the Ocean City and Middle Life-saving stations, keepers Harry Young and Edward Boyd saw the distress signals, and immediately used all at their disposal to begin rescue operations.

Their respective crews hurried to the stations, and the breeches buoy and surf boat were pressed into action. A scant 200 yards from the Ocean City boardwalk, the Sindia was pushing harder and deeper into the sand until her 26-foot draft was mocked by the shallow water and inviting bottom.

The Life-savers valiantly tried to shoot a breeches buoy to the ship, but one, and then two efforts failed. As daylight broke over the horizon, the surf boats were sent out, and after several trips to the Sindia and back to shore, all of the crewmen and officers were rescued.

The Sindia was said to have come to rest directly over the wreck of another British merchant ship that came ashore just before the American Revolution. This, coupled with the 200 tons of manganese ore aboard the Sindia, anchored the hulk forever to the beach.

The Sindia took on water profusely as soon as she settled into the sand. Much of the more perishable cargo was destroyed at this time, but salvage preparations were already underway just hours after the rescue of the men.

For all on shore, the beached vessel looked sound. It was oddly serene and statuesque as it rested just offshore. But beneath this model-like posture was a hull ravaged by its harsh collision with terra firma.

The madcap pilferage of the Sindia began almost immediately after the salvagers appointed by the ship's owners packed up and left. This indiscriminate raid on the ship's holds continued for months, and its legacy can still be felt.

Thousands of people hurried to the Ocean City beach to catch a glimpse of what became the shore's leading draw for several months.

Broadsides printed and distributed up and down the coast and in surrounding cities teased, "Come and See It!" The advertisements boasted, "SEE THREE DIVERS IN ACTION!"

The advertising worked. Gawkers who came to the city stood for hours on the beach and boardwalk, simply looking at the big bark, helpless on shore. Some painted the ship as it was that day, rooted in sand. Other used the lines and details of the four-master, but substituted a choppy sea for the Ocean City beach, placing the Sindia—at least on canvas—back in her rightful environment.

Several crewmen apparently opted to stay in the Ocean City area long after their rescue. Some feigned colds in order to gain the pity of druggists, who could issue alcoholic "remedies" in an otherwise dry city.

The gaudy treatment of the wreck of the Sindia had its serious and somewhat educational moments. The latest in underwater diving gear was used, and some folks who came to see the "three divers in action" had never before seen such equipment.

One advertisement in the Ocean City Daily Ledger attempted to dignify the wild times the Sindia was providing those on shore. "Come see the Sindia," it said, "come see nature's wonderful storehouse . . . such as ship worms, coral and hydrozoa!"

Never before, and perhaps never since, has Ocean City, New Jersey, seen anything like it.

The Sindia became a cottage industry up and down Ocean City's boardwalk. Some of the Japanese matting that was best preserved and dried became floor coverings for shore homes. Bales of bamboo were transformed into hundreds of fishing poles for area youngsters and the "curios" were sold for a dime, maybe twenty cents. Several massive, gold-trimmed, four-foot vases, now said to worth thousands of dollars, were sold from the Sindia for $30.

An entire shop popped up on the boardwalk, selling only the goodies gathered from the Sindia. One enterprising chemist from Camden bought a large quantity of some of the camphor oil aboard and sold it as "Sindia Oil and Linament."

Things got so bad that it's believed some bogus Sindia items began to infiltrate the profitable souvenir business. Profiteering photographers rallied to the scene, and within short order a series of post cards emerged on the market, as did countless other renderings of the Sindia as she began to waste away quickly in the surf.

Luckily, most of what was valuable historically was retrieved and has found its way into the "Sindia Room" of the Historical Museum. Even the enigmatic figurehead of the Sindia, a bearded Indian man, lost for several years after being hacked from the bowsprit, was returned to its rightful resting place in the early 1960s.

Elaborate salvage plans were announced from time to time over the decades, most notable the idea of one man who actually built a tram to the ship. The wind quickly claimed the tram's engine and put an end to that folly.

In the late 1930s, some residents suggested the deteriorating wreck be, somehow, removed from the shallow waters. Cooler heads prevailed, and it was pointed out to the detractors that the old wreck had actually become a part of the beach environment. Besides, it would be too expensive and dangerous to attempt to remove the huge scrap pile. What's more, the thing was still somewhat of a tourist attraction.

But what of the more serious side of things? What of the captain, the mate, the crewmen, and the circumstances that led to the wreck of the Sindia?

Was the weather alone the culprit in this near-tragic story that became a beachside burlesque? Were the claims of grog-gorged sailors and unattentive officers warranted?

The captain and mate were given their day in court. On February 7, 1902, they faced a board of inquiry at the British consulate in Philadelphia.

The court plodded through testimony and evidence, and came to the conclusion that yes, first mate George Stewart was negligent and, despite later protestations, under the influence of alcohol. Stewart was suspended for three months.

There were unsubstantiated stories that the first mate protected a captain who had become less than competent during the voyage. McKenzie, some said, was lackadaisical throughout the trip, and somehow the ship had lost valuable time. The captain, it was charged, had attempted to make up this time by placing his vessel in peril up the American coastline.

Indeed, the court declared that Captain McKenzie, whose record to that point was spotless, had "failed to exercise proper and seamanlike care and precaution."

The inquiry board further itemized the charge, noting that the Sindia was under too much canvas at the time of the grounding and not enough soundings were taken as the ship obviously was being blown off course.

Captain McKenzie died under mysterious circumstances six months after the decision of the court—almost to the day that his suspension meted out by the board would have been lifted.

His death, and the death of David Jackson Sr., the last surviving crewman of the Sindia in 1970, could have been the final words in the story of the great ship and its mystifying loss. But as long as the iron bones of the Sindia remain in the sand of the 17th Street beach, and as long as men continue to wonder about what's down there and come up with ways to find out, the legend of the Sindia will never, ever, fade away.

THE DISASTER THAT NEVER WAS

It could have been one of the worst tragedies ever in the history of the New Jersey shore. It had the potential of joining the Morro Castle as a ship's fire of catastrophic proportions.

But thankfully, in a way, it never happened.

Something really did happen that fateful December 21, 1905, but the incident caused more of a sensation on shore than out at sea.

The seas were rough and the wind whipped from the northeast as an ocean-going tug pulled its two barges on a northbound course barely two miles from the coast. One of the barges was named the "Reading," and the other was the "Ariel."

The Ariel was a former Norwegian schooner, a 996-ton vessel built in 1876. After logging a proud record as a merchant and passenger ship, she was sold to become a barge, as many similar schooners were.

Just off the shore of Ocean City, and for a still unknown reason, the Ariel (or more properly, the "Baker," as she had been renamed) caught fire.

The wind fueled the blaze, and the load of coal within her belly burst into a billowing, thick black smoke. From the shore, observers feared the worst.

Crews from Life-Saving stations at Chelsea, Longport and Ocean City scrambled to meet the blazing barge, totally unaware of what they might find.

It is said that women fainted on the Atlantic City boardwalk, firmly believing that it was a giant passenger liner fully involved in flames. Initial reports from men atop a tall hotel indicated they spotted the definite forms of human beings amid the inferno. Through powerful spyglasses, they ascertained it was a liner on fire just off the coast.

As the Life-Saving crews rowed frantically against the wind and the rolling surf, some 10,000 spectators lined the beaches from Ocean City to Atlantic City.

The drama continued the better part of the day. At last, toward dusk, the Life-Saving boats could be seen rowing back through the waves toward shore. Those on shore, certain that a major maritime disaster was taking place, were astounded at this development.

As the surfboats hit the beach, the weary Life-Savers told their tale. No passenger liner, just a barge. No carnage, just coal smoke.

WAR AT THE SHORE

"Captain, I'm sorry to do this, but it must be. You understand what it all means, of course. You will please clear your vessel as soon as possible for we are going to blow her up!"

With those firm, almost matter-of-fact words, an officer of the German navy announced that the freighter "Texel" would soon become a victim of one of the most incredible acts of war ever inflicted on Americans.

Although there have been bloodier and more bitterly contested incidents during the nation's wartime years, the bizarre chain of events during the first days of June, 1918, served to warn America and its merchant shipping fleet that it was quite vulnerable. This warning exacted a heavy toll of ship tonnage, and human lives.

June 2, 1918. The eastern shipping lanes, the New York Bight and the open sea itself were all peppered with ships sailing here and there, mostly unprepared for what was to happen. The combination of technology and raw-boned courage allowed the Kaiser's Unterseeboots to venture ominously close to American shores. Stealthily sneaking in from below the surface, these U-boats found easy pickings just off the coast of the United States. This is the story of some of the ships that went down closest to the southern New Jersey beaches.

Reports of maritime tragedies at the hands of German submarines filled the newspapers and the minds of Americans that first week of June. The "Edna," the "Hattie Dunn," "Wappaug," "Winneconne," the "Samuel W. Hathaway"— schooners and steamers lost to the U-boats' sneak attacks.

There were many more. The 1,360-ton schooner "Jacob H. Haskell," the "City of Columbus," and "Herbert L. Pratt" met their ends during this time.

In retrospect, it is interesting to note the fashion in which many of these vessels were destroyed by their attackers. Most historical accounts simply state that ships such as those mentioned above were "torpedoed" by German subs. This was not the case.

Aboard the schooner "Edward H. Cole," sailing off the North Jersey coast on June 2, someone noticed a submarine's conning tower in the water ahead. The captain of the Cole shouted out, "We are Americans," believing the sub was a "ours." From the sub come the reply, "We are Germans!" As the U-boat drew closer, its captain explained that the sailing ship was doomed.

"You have ten minutes to abandon your ship, and then we shall sink her," said the German.

"We can abandon her in five minutes," said the American.

The Cole's crew filed aboard lifeboats in an orderly manner, they rowed a safe distance away and watched as a gunner on the deck of the submarine aimed his weapon at the Cole's waterline, fired, and inflicted the fatal blows. The Cole was down in minutes.

The opening words of this chapter set the stage for the destruction of a much larger and much more important (in terms of cargo and ship tonnage) target of the German subs.

The "Texel" was a 5,000-ton former Holland-American Line freighter taken over by the United States government for wartime supply transport duty.

The weather during the Texel's voyage from Puerto Rico to New York City was calm and pleasant, and there was no reason to fear any aggression from the likes of the Germans. There simply was no indication that their U-boats were anywhere nearby.

The serenity of the cruise was shattered as during the late afternoon hours a gray-green object slowly rose out of the water and took a position near the Texel. In the sunny haze, the crewmen knew it was a submarine's "sail," and probably knew immediately that they were to become victims of the war.

A shell, and then another, exploded over the Texel's bow. Some Texel crewmen were hit by shrapnel, but not seriously wounded.

The two ships were quite close, close enough that at one time the captain of the Texel, K.B. Lowry of New York, feared that they would collide.

After the warning shots were fired across the freighter's bow, the German sub sent out a boarding party. The men from the U-boat went aboard the Texel, where the commander of the sub courteously requested the manifest and other papers of the freighter. He could afford to be courteous—the powerful guns of the sub were still trained on the Texel's deck!

The German captain discovered that the freighter was laden with some $2 million in sugar. As the two ships' masters discussed matters, demolition men from the sub were sizing up the freighter for the planting of TNT time bombs.

Charles Peterson, the Texel's chief engineer, recalled the boarding of his ship. "The lieutenant of the submarine was quite a prime fellow," he said. "He came aboard and extended his hand. Our captain looked at him a moment as if uncertain what to do. Then they shook hands.

"We noticed that he was a pleasant chap and I thought I recognized him as a former captain or first officer of a

Hamburg-American liner."

The dialogue between the two masters was brief, and both crews went about their business in rapid fashion. The Texel's men abandoned their ship and left it. The Germans returned to the deck of their submarine and watched as the seconds ticked away. At the prescribed time, the charges set by the crewmen earlier exploded and the Texel became a memory.

For some on board the freighter, this sort of thing was nothing new. Otto Ottoson, one of the Texel's deck hands, later said he was on three other ships sunk by German subs since 1914!

There were no casualties from this action. The crew spent some 36 hours in lifeboats, but eventually found their way to Atlantic City, where all 35 of them were landed safely.

The impudence of the German submarine captains during this time went far beyond the comparative gentility of the man who took the Texel as the spoils of war. Consider, if you will, the strange tale of the "Isabel B. Wiley."

She was a small, 779-ton, 160-feet wooden schooner on a short run from Newport News, Virginia, to New York. Aboard the ship was Captain H. Thomassen and a crew of seven when they were accosted by a U-boat.

At first, the pattern was the same as with the Texel. The German boarding party went to the Wiley and advised that they would destroy the vessel after the crew had time to abandon it. But this time, the crewmen were held captive and not allowed to set sail in lifeboats.

When the seven from the Wiley were taken custody inside the U-boat, they found themselves in company with 41 other victims of three subsequent U-boat encounters.

For a week, the Germans held the merchant ship crewmen, until they eventually released them in sight of oncoming ships and their eventual safe rescue.

During their captivity, Captain Thomassen of the Wiley is quoted as saying, the Germans tried to brainwash them and strike fear into their minds. Thomassen and others said the sub's captain was abrasive and cocky, bragging that the German subs, surface warships and planes would attack the United States within weeks and overcome their enemy.

The officers and crewmen of the sub also hailed their life in the German navy and particularly aboard Unterseeboots. As the week progressed, however, the Germans' brashness subsided a bit, and by the end of their ordeal, almost every one of the temporary prisoners was given a souvenir of their stay aboard the sub.

All of the action off the American coast during that first weekend of June appeared to be the result of a pack of four German U-boats. They had no trouble finding their prey, and the handful of attackers racked up hundreds of victims in their brief but brutal stay.

The subs dared to lay mines in the Chesapeake Bay. They toyed with the idea of venturing through Verrazano Narrows and into New York Harbor. Their vigor and thirst for Yankee tonnage was only dampened by a lack of fuel and explosives.

Of course, the U.S. Navy and Coast Guard's reaction to this sudden ambush activity was swift. Eastern ports were closed, sub chasers, flying boats and patrol vessels swarmed up and down the coast, and restrictions on shipping were imposed.

Unfortunately, all of this was too late for one of the fastest and finest liners that served the West Indies/New York route.

The Porto Rico Line's "Carolina" was bound from San Juan to New York City with 220 passengers and 120 crew members. There was a real fear at the offices of the Porto Rico Lines that the Carolina might be a target of the submarines, and after learning of the attacks of earlier in the day on June 2nd, Franklin D. Mooney, president of the firm, ordered the Carolina to divert from her straight course and go into sinuous steering in an attempt to confuse the Germans.

All seemed to be going well until about 6 p.m., when Captain T.R.D. Barbour of the Carolina was advised that the conning tower of an unidentified submarine was sighted just off the Carolina's beam.

Sure enough, the solemn-looking vessel lifted itself from the sea and crewmen rushed to the weather deck and to the gun mountings. The Carolina was a condemned ship.

Or was it? Because of her size and speed, the liner could very well have been prime for capture and return to Deutschland for conversion to warship. The German navy was in need of swift raiders, and the Carolina could have sufficed.

But the taking of the big ship was very similar to that of the others. The people aboard the ship were given ample time to leave, and the ship was destroyed.

As the sub approached, shells were fired across the Carolina's bow, and a boarding party was dispatched. Again, the captain of the U-boat was given qualified praise by those who were involved with the shipboard discussions.

Mrs. P.J. Hamilton, wife of the U.S. District court Judge based in San Juan, said, "the officer of the U-boat was as gentlemanly as one in his position could be."

She continued, "He told us that we did not have to hurry and no effort was made to hinder our getting away in the lifeboats. We had had life boat drill on the way up, and we all knew where we were to go. We all started for our respective boats and while everybody hurried, there did not seem to be any undue confusion. We got in and the lifeboats were lowered away."

After the Carolina was abandoned, the coup de grace was given. Mrs. Hamilton described it: "As we pushed from the side of the ship, the U-boat steamed around to the other side of the ship, and when the lifeboats had pulled out of the way, they began shelling the steamer. They poured six shots into her side. One of the shells must have been an explosive, for pretty soon she began to burn, and she was soon a roaring, seething mass of flames. She burned and remained afloat for probably an hour before she went down."

The passengers and crew of the Carolina were set adrift in ten lifeboats, and most were picked up soon by American and Russian merchant ships that passed by the scene of the sinking. Other lifeboats from the Carolina drifted out of the shipping lanes and toward the shore, but one was overturned by a storm south of Ocean City and more than two dozen lives were lost.

It was learned after the incident that but for quick thinking on the part of a certain segment of the passenger contingent, the episode could very well have taken on international scope.

Mrs. Charles S. Westbrook, a passenger on the Carolina, explained: "In spite of the fact that the Germans sank our ship we still have somewhat of a joke on them. On board there were a number of young United States Army officers. When they found that we had been halted by a submarine, every one of them sneaked away and took off their uniforms and puttees and thus they escaped any danger of being captured and taken prisoners on board the U-boat."

For the Ocean City-Atlantic City region, the most stirring story of all came with the arrival of a lifeboat full of Carolina survivors at the S. Carolina Ave. beach in Atlantic City on the day after the sinking.

The beach and boardwalk were both packed with an early-season crowd of sun worshippers and participants in a Shriners' convention. The Shriners band was playing on the boardwalk when the call came from lifeguards who spotted the craft with its ragged assemblage heading toward the beach.

As the boat was recognized as being from the Carolina, the mood on the shore turned from festive to wildly thankful. The Shrine band struck up the National Anthem and officials rushed to the aid of the survivors.

The survivors were given heroes' status in the city. They were taken to the Hotel Thurber at Atlantic and Massachusetts Avenues, for food and drink, and those who suffered, mentally and/or physically, were cared for at the Atlantic City Hospital.

Most of the survivors were remarkably well, considering their forty-hour adventure at sea. Oddly enough, every woman on board the boat was wearing a blue chambray shirt when they arrived on shore. Mrs. Westbrook explained that the shirts were actually found in a bundle floating by the lifeboat sometime during the night. A man on the lifeboat grabbed for the bundle with a boathook, and it was discovered that the package contained the dry shirts.

Mrs. Westbrook also described the events of the hectic night aboard the lifeboat. "We had a storm Sunday night," she said, "and we were fearful that we should have a rough time of it. But Monday morning dawned clear and warm.

"We saw two or three steamers' lights last night," she continued, "and we sent up rockets and shouted ourselves hoarse, but they soon passed out of sight and our hearts kind of dropped again. We saw a submarine chaser early this morning and one of the women took off her underskirt and put it aloft on a boathook. We shouted and shouted, but they evidently did not hear us, for they soon passed out of sight."

Finally, the woman recalled, the top of the Hotel Traymore, an Atlantic City landmark at that time, was spotted, and they rowed steadily toward it.

Once safe on shore, the people of Atlantic City threw their full spiritual and financial support behind the hapless victims of the sinking. The Shriners donated money for clothing and personal needs. The "Colored Division" of the Red Cross War Fund also raised $1,000, and more money and support came from dozens of other sources.

To be sure, the Carolina sinking, the deaths of those who never made it through the night, and the entire event's relationship to the much larger picture of World War I was tragic. But for young Carlotta Hamilton, daughter of the judge and his wife, it was something different. She was asked for her statement following the landing of the lifeboat in Atlantic City. She replied, "Why, as long as a Porto Rico boat had to be sunk by the Germans, I am glad that I was on it. I would not have missed it for anything in the world. When I know that all the people in the other boats are safe, that will remove every vestige of tragedy in the whole thing as far as I am concerned, and I shall be supremely happy."

At that time, quite obviously, she had no idea that so many of her shipmates had died.

DEATH IN THE FOG

When, as chronicled elsewhere in this volume, the Savannah Lines steamship firm was informed that its "City of Atlanta" was involved in a collision with the "Azua" in May of 1930, company officials could very well have shuddered.

Some could have been haunted by the spectre of another deep-water collision involving another of their ships almost exactly twelve years earlier.

The "City of Atlanta" was lucky. It remained afloat and survived the 1930 collision, while the "Azua" went to the bottom.

The May 1, 1918 collision of the Savannah Lines' "City of Athens" and a French naval cruiser, however, resulted in a devastating loss of life and the quick and painful loss of the steamer.

The mystery that to this day surrounds the incident is as thick and foreboding as the fog that was the major factor in the collision.

The setting for the tragedy couldn't have been better if Hollywood special-effects experts themselves had staged it.

The City of Atlanta pulled out of a New York harbor pier at about 8 p.m. that night and began her voyage to Savannah, Georgia. She sailed directly into a soupy fog bank that guarded the south Jersey cape and loomed off the Ocean City shore like a curtain on the horizon.

There is some controversy as to the light scheme of the steamer that night. Initial reports indicated that the City of Atlanta was fully aglow with all lights as she slipped into the fog. A report filed by company officials following the collision ascertained that the ship's lights were dimmed, in accordance with the wartime footing observed along the eastern seaboard.

It doesn't really matter. The fact is that the 3,648-ton vessel left port with 135 men, women and children aboard and only 68 of them lived to tell their tragic tales.

Those tales were sketchy, at best, from most of the passengers. The vast majority of them were already in their staterooms and retired for the night when the collision took place.

Those in the crew, however, may have told more coherent and complete stories. And, there could have been many, many versions, as an astonishing 33 crew members survived the crash. Only 35 passengers lived.

The demise of the City of Athens was quick, indeed. It was said that during the mayhem following the initial ramming, those trying to save themselves or others literally looked around for the big steamer and it was gone.

Witnesses say the bow of the city of Athens was barely visible from the bridge on that fateful night. Suddenly, despite the most vigilant efforts of the lookouts, a French navy cruiser plunged from the fog and directly into the port bow of the City of Athens. There was no warning, and no time whatsoever to avoid the collision.

Passengers aboard the American ship were shaken from their beds as the steamer heaved to a heavy starboard list. Within a few minutes, she started to roll, and after seven minutes was all but gone.

The crew leaped into action, but found the going rough, given the circumstances at hand. The time factor was but one vexing problem. There were also reports (also refuted later by Savannah Lines officials) that lifeboats were not ready, davits were malfunctioning and ropes were brittle.

Again, it mattered not in the haste and confusion that marked the sinking of the liner.

In fact, most lifeboats were capsized by the initial blow inflicted on the City of Athens by the French warship, "La Glorie."

It is ironic that aboard the American passenger ship was a large contingent of French marines and sailors. They, along with another group of American marines headed for Parris Island for training, were among the bravest in the mad scramble for salvation.

On board the "La Glorie," men rallied to rescue those who could be seen in the thick fog. Searchlights from the cruiser cut swaths of milky light through the dark and crewmen groped through the fog and the choppy seas, listening for shouts and moans from those hoping to be saved. The French ship's bugler blew a plaintive call into the night to serve as an audible beacon for anyone who could manage to swim toward the ship.

There were, no doubt, many heroes that night. But the annals of this shipwreck maintain but one name—that of the City of Athens' wireless operator, F.J. Doherty. He knew with the first massive crash of the French cruiser's bow into the side of the steamer that his ship was doomed. He probably knew that he, too, was to die. Still, he maintained his post to the very end, tapping out a pointless, fruitless S.O.S. until the fires silenced his wireless and the seas silenced him.

THE FLOUR WRECK

As you will note throughout this book, many of the shipwrecks in the sea off the coast of Ocean City have been given fanciful nicknames.

These range from the "Pet Wreck," the "Pig Iron Wreck" and the "$25 Wreck" to the "Mud," "Bell" and "Stone" wrecks. Most are but phantoms in the seagoing history of this portion of the New Jersey coastline. The actual names of the ships that rest on the sandy bottom of the ocean have been obscured by time, and most divers and fishermen who ply their trades on and over these underwater attractions know little or nothing about what lies down there.

One of these monickered wrecks is known as the "Flour Wreck." Although it is relatively common knowledge that the ship that rests in 70 feet of water almost due east of Ocean City was the American freighter, "Almirante," few people may realize the events that sent her to her watery grave.

As was the case with many or most of the notable sea tragedies off this coast, the weather was dank and foggy, it was the middle of the night, and two ships were heading on a collision course.

It was just after two in the morning on Friday, September 6, 1918 when the Almirante was headed along the coastline with her cargo filling the 5,000-ton steel ship to capacity.

Coming in the opposite direction was the government freighter Hiasko, northbound with potatoes and a general bill of lading.

Reports of the day indicated that neither ship was using accepted fog precautions despite the thick bank of heavy mist that enveloped them. It could very well be that both captains threw fog precautions to the wind, owing to another potentially dangerous situation. It was the midst of the first world war, and there was always the risk of enemy warships and submarines entering the local coastal waters.

With little or no warnings, the two ships continued on their courses, unaware that tragedy was imminent.

Although lookouts kept watch on the bows of both ships, listening diligently for the sound of an oncoming vessel, the fog was so uncompromising that even the most alert lookout could not have prevented the accident.

The Almirante carried a large crew of 85 men. Many were in their hammocks or beds at that hour of the morning, when their solitude was shattered.

The Hiasko plowed through the choppy seas and emerged from the fogbank in an instant. Lookouts aboard the Almirante screamed a warning, but to no avail. In horror, those on watch aboard the Almirante watched as the Hiasko's prow sliced into the Almirante with a horrible force. The steel bulkheads of the Almirante were cut and crushed in an instant.

The men of the Almriante had little time to consider their options. Seconds after impact, it was clear that the ship was sinking. The men leaped to save their lives, and most did.

It's reported that it took only four minutes for the Almirante to slither beneath the surface of the sea. In a tangle of wreckage from the big freighter's decks, 80 men fought for survival in the deadly sea. The Hiasko backed off and positioned itself for rescue operations.

At the same time, an S.O.S. was tapped out and received at Life-saving stations on shore. These vigilant crews assembled and sped by powerboat to the scene.

The Life-savers arrived on time to help with the rescue of the Almirante's crewmen, and as the survivors were taken aboard the Hiasko, they were given coffee and dry clothing, and their numbers were counted.

By the time the rescue was deemed complete, at about noontime that day, it was determined that four men were missing from the ranks of the Almirante crew. One dead body was plucked from the wreckage, and 80 were saved.

It was felt that the four who could not be found had died in the opening seconds of the episode. They were probably asleep in the crew's quarters and never had a chance of survival.

The search was called off, and the Hiasko, although damaged about the bow by the collision, continued to New York.

The dead seamen were added to the ranks of those who lost their lives in unpredictable seas off Ocean City, and the name of the Almirante was etched into the maritime history of the region.

And, oh yes—although the present day wreck site is more commonly called the "Flour Wreck," it should be noted that the Almirante, a United Fruit Company vessel, was carrying a cargo of fruit, not flour!

THE PHANTOM BARGE

Sometimes, in the murky depths and often murkier historical records that harbor shipwrecks, fact and fantasy intertwine.

Sketchy contemporary documentation, fading memories and strong underwater currents can result in what seems to be or is said to be never really being at all.

This could very well be the case with a shipwreck in some 55 feet of water 18 miles off the coast of Ocean City.

There is little doubt that there is a wreck at that location. Most accounts say it is that of the "John L. Martino."

But is it?

The strange tale of the John L. Martino began with her birth in the storied shipyards of Bath, Maine. The ship, christened as the "Winnegance," rolled out of the J.G. Morse yards in 1890, her 213 tons splashing into the cold Maine waters bound for coasting the eastern shipping routes.

The sturdy three-masted schooner performed yeoman service for nearly four decades until it met a rather ignoble fate on the seas off Ocean City.

Or did it?

Even in contemporary headlines, the Martino was dubbed a "MYSTERY SHIP" and "PHANTOM BARGE." It was the subject of legal tests of the laws of salvage at sea, and the exact fate of the Martino is unclear to this day.

Most references to wrecks off the Ocean City shore acknowledge that the John L. Martino, a schooner, sank about 18 miles out on August 20, 1928. This much, research shows, is totally incorrect.

The Atlantic City Press reported in its August 20 edition

that there was a strange occurrence off the coast of Ocean City the previous day. "A phantom ship, unknown and unlisted in marine agencies, shrouded with mystery as to its destination or its port of embarkation, with tattered sails, its cabin swept clean of charts, nautical papers and compasses, and suspicioned of being a rum-runner and the scene of a crime . . . was found drifting about 18 miles off the coast," the story began.

The ship, described as a three-masted schooner, was discovered by Francis Widerstrom, master of the fishing boat, "Victoria," out of Anglesea. In coming weeks, Capt. Widerstrom would probably wish he'd never laid eyes on the derelict.

Widerstrom boarded the ship, discovered that it was named the "John L. Martino," and was confused about its status. The tables and compartments were strangely devoid of any seagoing equipment, and all that remained in the cabin was an odd assortment of women's clothing, including a kimono, one slipper and underwear.

The holds of the ship were filled with a jumble of lumber, and the schooner's masts were tumbled and down. Below decks, the lifeless vessel was beginning to take on water, and it appeared for all intents to be within the bounds of "fair game" for salvage.

Captain Widerstrom decided to tow the schooner back to Anglesea and claim it under the maritime laws. But a strange thing happened to Widerstrom on the way to the port. Along came a Coast Guard patrol boat.

The Coast Guard personnel saw things a bit differently. They saw an abandoned schooner, stripped of anything valuable, and its cargo area jammed willy-nilly with lumber.

Exactly what had happened? Exactly what mission was the John L. Martino on when it was abandoned? There was too much suspicion and too many unanswered questions. The Coast Guard wanted answers, and wanted the schooner at one of its stations.

Capt. Widerstrom vehemently protested the Coast Guard's claims to the ship. He said it was a derelict, he had found it, and by law, it was his.

The Coast Guard, however, had the last say. They cut the

towing line Capt. Widerstrom's crew had placed on the Victoria and rigged their own line. They towed it back to their station at Cape May, with two of the Victoria's crewmen aboard the Martino. They simply refused to "give up the ship," and protested by not leaving it.

The confusion over rights to the vessel widened within the following days when it was discovered that the Martino was a ship with an owner, and that owner wanted it back. Legal proceedings against Widerstrom were begun by the ship's owner in Brooklyn, and conferences between Widerstrom, the owners and the Coast Guard failed to bear any fruit. The captain steadfastly maintained that the derelict was his by the right of nautical salvage law.

Soon enough, the facts behind the mysterious schooner began to surface. No, it was not engaged in rum-running, and no, there were no heinous crimes committed aboard before all disappeared.

The John L. Martino left a southern port on July 28, 1928, with a cargo of lumber bound for New England. On August 12, as the schooner passed the coast off Ocean City, it began to take on water. No one aboard, including Capt. R. Horsman, knew exactly what happened. Some suspected that the ship struck a large, partially-submerged object and a hole was punched below the water line.

The ship was in trouble, but not sinking rapidly. The master, his wife, and six crewmen stayed aboard until the British steamer "Mayaro" came along. Also on a northerly course, the steamer noticed the smaller schooner in trouble amid the choppy sea and ventured closer to help.

In the process of rescuing those aboard the Martino, the Mayaro lost its number two lifeboat, but eventually all were brought to safety. The seas had begun to take its toll on the schooner, however, as its masts were crumbling and water continued to gush in.

During the rescue, the schooner's master managed to take with him anything of value, leaving behind the few women's garments, and a profound mystery.

It was one week later that the Martino's aimless hulk was discovered by Capt. Widerstrom, all the more forlorn and weatherbeaten.

What became of the Martino? All efforts to determine its ultimate fate fell short of success. If nothing else, though, it appears certain that it did not, as generally accepted, sink on August 20, 1928.

THE DEATH SHIP "AZUA"

A dense fog shrouded the New Jersey coastline on May 14, 1930. Still, ships continued along their courses, tightly hugging the treacherous shoreline.

The "City of Atlanta," a Savannah Lines steamer, and the "Azua," a 664-ton schooner, were both southbound that night when destiny brought them together in a tragic encounter.

It was shortly after midnight when a wireless operator at the Radio Marine Corporation in New York reported the signal from the City of Atlanta: It had just collided with an unidentified schooner south and east of Great Egg Inlet.

The extremely adverse weather conditions of that night, coupled with the darkness and relatively primitive communication systems of the day, made it initially impossible for Captain

John H. Diehl of the City of Atlanta to reckon what vessel was struck, and what the extent of damage might have been.

When the fog lifted and the facts were sorted out, however, it became painfully obvious that the collision was fatal.

For Captain Diehl, the crashing sound of the collision must have been a haunting clatter. Just five years before, his "City of Rome" steamer smashed into the submarine "S-51" off Clock Island. Thirty-five lives were lost, and Captain Diehl was accused of misconduct and negligence. He was subsequently acquitted of those counts, but a veil of suspicion had followed him to his next command.

Aboard the Azua, there was no time to consider past glories or tragedies. The giant steamer slashed into the small schooner and almost immediately sent her to the bottom.

Bound for Bermuda with a cargo of coal, the Azua was a sturdy ship built in the storied yards of Bath, Maine. She was the pride and lifeblood of J.A. McLean, who both owned and captained the 12-year old vessel.

The Azua's first mate was Robert Christian, who resided on the fashionable Fifth Avenue in New York City. These two men, along with a sailor identified only as "Palmer," were to go down in death with the Azua on that tragic night.

As the City of Atlanta's bow was ripping into the schooner's side, those aboard both vessels knew the Azua was doomed. No doubt, McLean and Christian fought valiantly to save their ship.

The larger and surviving craft immediately launched a boat to rescue those who may have lived through the disaster. A handful of men were seen struggling in the waves, and a radio message was sent back to New York indicating that all aboard the Azua were saved. This later proved to be a terribly inaccurate report.

Indeed, three men were helped aboard the lifeboat and onto the City of Atlanta. Sailors Pedro Cattill and John Smith and Fred Tulford, identified as the "negro cook," were saved, but there were no signs of the captain, mate or the other crew member.

For about seven hours, until dawn on May 14, the City of Atlanta remained in the vicinity to search for the others. As morning broke and fog lifted, however, it was ascertained that nothing but bits and pieces of flotsam were left to mark the grave of the Azua.

Today, that wreckage rests in 120 feet of water, about 25 miles from Great Egg Inlet. It is but one of dozens of wrecks that dot the bottom of the shipping lanes off the coast of Ocean City.

THE FALL OF THE "FALL RIVER"

The phrase, "gales of November" stirs fear in the hearts of mariners both on the sea and in America's Great Lakes. It is during these unpredictable and savage storms that many of the sea tragedies of lore and legend have occurred.

This story hardly can be counted among those, but it is typical of the kind of work-a-day wrecks that have been common along the south Jersey coast.

The tug, "Eureka," was braving a November 1, 1932 gale with three Martin Corp. barges bound from Norfolk, Va., to Boston. Heavily laden with coal, one of the barges, the "Fall River," began to leak somewhere due east of Ocean City. Through a full night and another day, the four-man crew aboard the Fall River struggled to keep the barge afloat. Raging winds and rain made their fight against fate all the more perilous, and luckily, the crew of the Atlantic City Coast Guard Station noticed their problems.

Quickly, a cutter sped from Absecon Inlet to the whitewater sea in an attempt to save the men aboard the fast-sinking barge.

By late afternoon, the men of the barge were taken aboard the Coast Guard boat and given refuge ashore.

On the shore, the storm continued to wreak havoc with the land. Roads were flooded, buildings were flattened by tornado-like winds, and damage estimates went into the hundreds of thousands of dollars.

But for the four men of the Fall River, it could have been much, much worse!

A TRAGIC SUNDAY

It couldn't have happened at a worse time.

August, 1933. The nation was pulling itself up by the bootstraps. Newspaper stories told of a renewed strength of the nation's banking system, optimistic words from Hyde Park, N.Y., where President Roosevelt was reviewing the apparent success of his "New Deal," and the start of the slaughter of 5 million hogs—the signal of a recovery on the nation's troubled hog farms.

Rudy Vallee and Alice Faye were injured in a Bridgeville, Delaware, automobile accident and all-out war was declared on gangsters like Machine Gun Kelly and Al Capone. In Atlantic City, a group of investors was looking for a site for a proposed horse race track.

The mood of the nation was generally upbeat, despite its many deep problems.

On Sunday, August 20, 1933, in particular, all was well in the rich fishing banks just off Great Egg Inlet. There was no indication early on that the day would be etched in the annals of Ocean City as one of the most tragic ever.

By mid-day, there were an estimated 100 small-to-medium sized fishing and cruising boats off the coast between Absecon and Avalon.

The water was dotted with craft ranging from rowboats to yachts. Some folks were fishing, some simply relaxing under a cloudy but calm Sunday sky.

With comparatively primitive weather forecasting and warning techniques, no one could foretell the swift and deadly course of a tropical depression that was brewing in the West Indies. The Ocean City pleasure fleet took to the offshore waves in all its glory that Sunday morning, and the sport fishing flotilla likewise cruised out of Great Egg Inlet.

It was late August, and the water temperature was finally dropping. At last, fishing was good. This quest for the bounty of the sea, however, proved to be fatal.

All morning, there were hints of an oncoming storm. Still, there were no gale or small craft warnings, so the rising heights of the waves and the misty precipitation could be overlooked.

On the shore, there was mounting evidence that something was to occur. It was the calm before the storm. By mid-afternoon, some veteran sea watchers knew that the hundreds of people out there may be in danger.

One man, Captain James Allen of Ocean City, took immediate action. Captain Allen owned a fleet of five fishing party boats that were out off the Ocean City shoreline on that afternoon. Sensing trouble, he chartered an airplane and flew to the fishing banks where his fleet was operating.

As he passed overhead, he dropped corked bottles attached to life preservers. Inside each bottle was a note instructing the captains of the fishing boats to make for Cold Spring Harbor because of the expected storm.

Other fishing and cruise boats were not as lucky.

In what was described as "one of the strangest occurrences ever noted in these waters" in an Atlantic City Press story, the tropical storm slammed into the South Jersey shoreline with unparalleled fury and surprise.

The stiff winds and heavy rains were confined to a narrow belt that slithered up the coastline, just offshore, like an unpredictable killer cobra.

On the mainland, there was no cause for concern. Indeed, just ten miles offshore, the weather was quite calmer. But in that singular river of a storm just off the beaches of Ocean City, all hell was breaking loose!

Waves reached thunderous proportions and steady downpours dumped inches of rain within minutes. Up and down the coast, every available Coast Guard man and vessel was pressed into action.

In the Atlantic City-Ocean City area, the Coast Guard emergency armada consisted of a half-dozen speedboats, a like number of surf boats, two patrol boats and a destroyer. From late afternoon to late evening, these boats and ships saw unbroken service.

What's more, several private yachts and fishing boats were sent out to aid in rescue efforts. Even the "Miss Atlantic City," the oversized tourist speedboat, sped into the storm.

Frantic tales of heroism and death returned to anxious folks on shore as each boat made its way back to safety. Some, of course, never did find their way to harbor.

The toll for those from Ocean City was heavy. Several boats out of the city were lost, and dozens of men, women and children who sailed from ocean City were caught in the maelstrom.

As the storm doubled back onto land, its fury wreaked havoc on shorefront properties. The Ocean City boardwalk suffered damage, as did bulkheads that were only recently installed to protect against and withstand the most severe of storms.

The wind and rain continued incessantly for several days, flooding streets and tearing trees from their roots. Several streets in Ocean City were flooded, and it was estimated that the Kassab Building, then an apartment building along the Boardwalk near Fourth Street, was pushed back a full six inches by the rushing floodwaters.

What was left of the summer season was all but ruined. The storm had done its swift and certain damage, and for thousands of Ocean City residents and visitors, that certain Sunday in August, 1933, would never be forgotten.

S.O.S. . . . S.O.S.

"S.O.S. . . . S.O.S. . . . COLLIDED WITH UNKNOWN SHIP . . . BIG HOLE IN NUMBER ONE HOLD FORWARD . . . AFIRE . . . OTHER SHIP SINKING!"

This frantic message sizzled through the airwaves on the night of Saturday, January 17, 1942. Fifteen miles due east of Ocean City, a high drama on the high seas was playing out.

The coastal towns of New Jersey had a right to be a bit skitterish about what happened beyond their shores. The time was the month after the surprise attack on Pearl Harbor. Already the Nazi U-Boats were preying on coastal shipping, and although most information was withheld by the Navy Department, it was well known that several freighters and tankers fell victim to German torpedoes—some in full view of the beaches.

Ironically enough, on January 19, 1942, a story made the front page of the Atlantic City PRESS under the headline: "Alive With Subs." "The public relations office of the Norfolk Naval Operating Base announced last night that a merchant ship had been torpedoed and sunk off the Atlantic coast. The name of the craft, the location of the sinking and time of the torpedoing were not made public," the story read, continuing, " . . . survivors, including two Americans, who reached here yesterday said enemy submarines were 'almost as thick as catfish' in the waters where they were attacked."

There was death and destruction, and the horror of warfare, just off the coast of New Jersey's prime resort towns.

This wartime footing contributed directly to the spectacular collision of the freighters "San Jose" and "Santa Elisa."

The San Jose, a 3,358-ton United Fruit Company freighter

loaded with coffee from Latin America bound for the United States, was steaming placidly on an unusually balmy January Saturday.

As darkness set in, the captain of the San Jose complied with Navy Department orders to dim all lights and knew full well that all other vessels around the San Jose were doing the same.

One of those ships was the Grace Line Santa Elisa, which would prove to be the ruin of the San Jose.

It was in the early evening, at about 8, when the San Jose and Santa Elisa met on a collision course.

The radioman aboard the Santa Elisa tapped out his S.O.S. moments after the two ships plowed into each other. Flares were shot high into the sky, illuminating the horrifying scene and attracting attention to the plight of the two big freighters.

One freighter was much bigger than the other, and at more than 7,600 tons, the Santa Elisa was to fare much better than the San Jose.

Almost instantly upon contact with the Santa Elisa, the San Jose began to founder. A massive hole was ripped in her forward section, below the water line. She quickly took on water and began to slip under the surface of the sea. The San Jose went to its watery grave some 66 feet under water even before the first rescue boats arrived.

An incredible display of visual and audible effects ensued. Flames shot from the Santa Elisa as fire toyed with her cargo of oil. On shore, observers reported a resounding echo of explosions and a bright flash that mushroomed into the night sky.

At Ocean City, distress signal rockets and flares were clearly visible as the Santa Elisa fought for its life. Coast Guard vessels were dispatched immediately.

The first vessels to come to the aid of the stricken freighters, however, were other merchant steamers, "Charles L. O'Connor" and "Wellhart." Both were cruising nearby and received the S.O.S. from the Santa Elisa, and both arrived after the San Jose slipped below.

The rescue efforts began as men from the Wellhart and O'Connor searched the dark sea for survivors. Ironically, the flames from the burning Santa Elisa aided in the search, and by midnight, most survivors were given refuge on the merchant ships.

Coast Guard crewmen from Ocean City, under the command of a Boatswain's Mate Jennings, were among the first guardsmen to arrive. They stayed on the scene until about 1 a.m., when it was apparently confirmed that all crewmen from both ships were safe.

Many of those survivors were suffering from exposure, with some spending as much as three hours in the icy water. Most were so weak that they had to be hoisted aboard the rescue vessels by slings.

The Santa Elisa, heavily damaged and scalded by the intense flames, was eventually beached off Brooklyn, where its cargo was gingerly removed. She was listing to port, suffering from a large gash in her bow.

The San Jose is today deep in the sea off Ocean City. An occasional diver may go below to explore what's left of the ill-fated ship, but basically the underwater carcass is home to mussels and an occasional lobster.

There is little doubt that the dimming of lights aboard these ships travelling the busy shipping lanes of the east coast contributed to the collision. But, in the time period of the San Jose-Santa Elisa incident, several tankers and freighters were torpedoed by German submarines fairly close to the New Jersey shore.

THE NAZIS SINK THE VARANGER

Today, fishermen call it a haven for blues, cod and tuna. They call it the "28 Mile Wreck" because it is just about 28 miles from the Ocean City beach, and indeed exactly 28 miles from Great Egg Inlet.

The wreck has a name. It is the "Varanger," a well-preserved, deep-water hulk with one of the most fascinating stories of any sunken ship off the coast of New Jersey.

Little has been recorded about the vital statistics of the Varanger. Its very displacement has been variously reported as anywhere between 5,500 to 14,000 tons. What is known about the vessel, however, is that it was one of the first casualties of daring and dangerous German Unterseeboot activities in the east coast shipping lanes of the United States during World War II.

It was the second round of such bold and barbarous attacks by German submarines on American shipping. A spurt of destruction during the first world war touched the shipping lanes, but the audacity of the Nazi U-boat captains reached new heights.

The deep canyons just off shore provided adequate hiding space for the subs as they waited to attack any merchant vessel they could find. The finding was relatively easy. During the first months of American involvement in the war, the merchantmen sailed under peacetime rules. Masthead, range and running lights glowed into the night, channel markers were beacons guiding the way to inlets, and radio messages crackled over the air waves.

Nobody knows how many subs plied the coastal waters in the first months of 1942. Some cruised alone, in groups of two or three, or in larger "Wolfpacks" and wherever they went, destruction followed.

It's estimated that as many as 400 ships fell victim to the Nazi aggression close to our shores. Reportedly, the pickings were so plentiful for the U-boats that the only reason they held up on the carnage was that they ran short of fuel and torpedoes.

The American defenses were down. The fleet was unprepared for such close-in action. Many capital ships were on assignment in other theaters, and the lend-lease agreement with England had decimated eastern fleets. Only a handful of Nazi subs were eventually destroyed until the coasts could be properly guarded.

That time was far too late for the Varanger.

The big tanker was northbound to New York on January 25, 1942, her tanks gorged with oil. Perhaps her captain knew of at least one recent sinking and several threats against eastern shipping. Perhaps precautions of some kind were made to prevent such misfortune for the Varanger.

Whatever, it was an unremarkable voyage up until about ten minutes after three o'clock in the morning on January 25. Captain Karl Horne, a 42-year old Norwegian who married a Pennsylvania girl and settled in Philadelphia, was asleep in his bunk. The Varanger's 41-member crewmen were going about their watch duties, and the ship was nearly due east of Ocean City when the lives of these men were changed forever.

Silently, swiftly, and order was given. Somewhere just under the surface of the sea, a Nazi captain gave the order to fire. A torpedo sped on its way into the Varanger's side.

At 3:10 a.m., the underwater missile ripped into the port bow of the Norwegian tanker, exploding a fatal gash in her deck, destroying two lifeboats and knocking out the radio shack. With this first blow, the ship was doomed. Without radio communications, any hope of rescue was a long way off.

Within a minute or two, it was painfully obvious that the Varanger was doomed. Captain Horne was shaken from his bed by the first explosion and awoke to stand in ankle-deep oil, gushing into the compartments and passageways like blood from a severed artery.

The crew members barely had enough time to scramble for their salvation when another torpedo slammed into the ship. Within moments, yet another "fish" opened yet another hole in the tanker's port side.

Those men on the bow section at the time of the first hit were virtually trapped. They were forced to brave freezing waters and oozing oil to reach their lifeboats. They survived, but suffered greatly.

In fact, somehow all the men of the Varanger lived to tell their tale. this, despite the fact that the first rescue craft didn't arrive until after sunrise.

Witnesses reported that the sinking of the ship took all but fifteen minutes. She went down ablaze, her liquid cargo set on fire by the explosions. In the hazy, smoky glow, the crewmen watched as the submarines surfaced. One, and then two U-boats slipped through the waves, and circled their fallen prey like vultures circle carrion. Huddled aboard their pathetic lifeboats in various stages of fear and exposure, the Varanger's men silently witnessed this spectacle. Their captain had ordered them to remain silent, fearing that any insults hurled at Nazi sailors on deck might result in retaliatory attacks on the lifeboats themselves.

As the eerie death light of the Varanger dimmed, the German subs slinked back to their murky depths. The survivors of the incident were alone, freezing, and frightened.

For some four hours, the men—all but two were Norwegians—bobbed and rolled in the January sea.

Little did anyone on shore know that what they heard, and in some cases, felt at 3:10 a.m. was the sinking of a tanker just off their coast. It was reported, though, that windows rattled and a concussion could be felt from Ocean City to Sea Isle City.

Dewey Monchetti, a 57-year old Sea Isle City fisherman, and his 20-year old nephew, John Monchetti, were well aware of the mysterious explosion early that morning. They had just put out for early morning cod fishing from the 32-foot San Gennaro.

They reached the fishing banks 22 miles out at about 7:30

that morning. After setting their lines, they noticed small sailboats on the horizon. Drifting toward them were the lifeboats of the Varanger.

As the lifeboats, filled beyond capacity with the 41 men of the tanker, drifted closer, the Monchettis could see that those aboard were coated with oil and in very poor condition.

They maneuvered their fishing boat closer to the lifeboats and prepared to help in any way they could. With the San Gennaro was a sister boat, the Eileen, captained by Dominic Costantino. He, too, participated in the rescue.

The survivors were taken to Sea Isle City, where Defense Council, Red Cross and local church and civic groups were assembled to lend assistance. Local physicians tended to the more seriously affected men.

The story is not without certain ironies. There was one casualty of the sinking. The Varanger's mascot was killed when it leaped from a crewman's arms into the sea. It was a dog. A Dachshund.

Even more incredible is the story of Dewey Monchetti, the veteran of 43 years as a fisherman and captain of the San Gennaro. His brother drowned in a fishing accident a dozen years before the Varanger incident. But at one time in Dewey's life, he, too, was nearly killed at sea.

He was a crewman aboard a freighter, when the big ship ran into trouble at sea and sank. All hands, including Dewey Monchetti, were saved. By the crew of a German ship!

1942—THE CARNAGE CONTINUES

The sinking of the "Varanger" was just the beginning of the open warfare on the American coast between Nazi submarines and American shipping.

Gradually, many merchant vessels were outfitted with gun mounts that could serve as a defensive weapon, but this proved to be a token measure, at best.

On the mainland, Americans were making sacrifices as the war effort broadened and began to stretch the nation's resources rather thin. By late winter, such vital supplies as gasoline, sugar, tires, automobiles and even bicycles and typewriters were rationed, with the promise of many more items to be limited as well.

The South Jersey tourist season appeared to be doomed, especially in resort towns such as Ocean City that were inaccessible by direct train travel. Already, rationing of gasoline was keeping most people away from non-essential travel and even sightseeing bus excursions were banned.

The Nazi navy was on America's doorstep. The daily papers and radio news reports were peppered with dispatches from "An Atlantic Port" as a veil of secrecy was dropped over most maritime movements.

Not only the United States suffered during this dark period. In the winter months of 1942, various allies' merchantmen were targets of he German U-boats that ventured into the eastern shipping routes. One of the most notable victims was the Brazilian ship "Cayru."

The 5,100-ton was built in Philadelphia and christened as the "Scanmail" in 1919. Twenty years later, she was sold to the Lloyd-Brasiliero Line.

On March 8, 1942, the Cayru was on a voyage from Buenos Aires to New York City, coasting some 35 miles off the New Jersey shores on a relatively calm evening. All precautions against possible submarine attacks were being taken.

A Nazi U-boat, presumed to be the U-404, made a mockery out of these precautions when it struck silently with a torpedo aimed at the Cayru's bow.

But instead of a deafening and death-dealing explosion, all that was heard was the plaintive clunk of metal against metal. The torpedo, as was the case all too often for the Nazis, was a dud.

The thud was loud enough to alert the crew of the Cayru to the fact that their ship was in the crosshairs of a sub captain's aim. Immediately, the lifeboats were launched and the passengers and crew began an orderly, if not hasty, abandonment.

Within minutes, the sub fired another underwater bullet at the Cayru. This time, the torpedo slammed into the midships area and inflicted a mortal wound.

The impact of the second explosion split the Cayru in two and sent her remains down rapidly.

All of the passengers and crew members left the ship before the second hit, and it was hoped that all could survive the rough seas and freezing water temperatures long enough to find refuge on shore.

As the hours and days passed, though, it became clear that the attack on the Cayru would become a disaster. In all, 32 of those on board the vessel on March 8 survived, but more than 50 others perished, presumably lost when March gales swamped their lifeboats.

Brazilian authorities were livid with rage over the unprovoked attack on another of their ships. The South American nation put immediate clamps on the activities of German nationals there, and took over all German property within its borders. Another nation had entered the hostilities, as the result of an incident just off the shore of Ocean City.

Less than a week later, another major coastal steamer became the target and victim of U-404, this time less than ten miles from the beach.

The supplies had to get through, no matter how dangerous the duty for the brave merchant seamen. All too often, these intrepid sailors put their lives on the line for the unglamorous, often thankless task they chose.

Ship's master Grover D. Clark was bringing his 7,600-ton freighter "Lemuel Burrows" up the coast from Norfolk to New York City with a load for the Koppers Coal Company. The Camden-built, 25-year old ship was owned by the Mystic Steamship Co. of Boston, and 34 men were serving aboard her on her last cruise, March 14, 1942.

The Burrows was hugging the coast, barely eight miles out when it happened. At about 2 a.m., with no inkling that it was about to take place, a German torpedo ripped through the freighter's plating on the starboard bow. Several minutes passed, and as the crew was abandoning the marked ship, another "fish" exploded—this time of the port side, midships.

Nearly all of the crew were off the Burrows when yet another torpedo struck. The damage was already done, and the Burrows was listing precariously, slipping steadily under the waves. The swell created by the third torpedo swamped several of the lifeboats filled with men frantically trying to escape, and there were many casualties.

When all was sorted out, only 14 of the 34 on board were survivors. The Nazi submarine captain, while not necessarily bloodthirsty for human lives, had achieved his mission of sinking many more tons of vital coal bound for the American war machine.

Further research into the matter provides some solace for those Americans who look for such a thing during wartime. Almost a year after its brutal attacks on east coast shipping, U-404 was bombed in the North Atlantic and sunk. All on board were killed.

The assault on the maritime lifelines continued until American defenses could be bolstered. Along the way, several more ships were sunk by Nazi subs. The "Rio Tercero," a 4,800-ton

Argentine freighter headed to Buenos Aires from New York City, was torpedoed off Ocean City on June 22, 1942, and others, accounts of which were confidential at the time and irretrievable today, remain largely nameless.

Even among the small craft that patrolled the coastline there were accidental casualties. The "YP 387" shows up on some wreck charts of the South Jersey shore. This was a Yard Patrol boat that operated out of the 3rd Naval District in New York. It went down on May 20, 1942 after a collision with an unidentified craft or obstruction.

In a sense, America seemed to be still reeling from the attack on Pearl Harbor and its Lend-Lease agreement with Britain and Russia. At the same time, Admiral Karl Donitz, who commanded the German submarine forces, threw all he could at American coastal activities.

War records reveal that in January, 1942, about 145,000 tons of shipping were claimed by the U-boats. In February, 36 ships and 192,000 tons were destroyed. The total soared to 47 ships and 275,000 tons in March.

This action off the coast, and indeed within sight of Ocean City and other shore points, became another "front" for the American military.

The coast was difficult to protect, especially with the depleted number of ships and patrol craft available. Convoy-style ship movements were organized, and British ships were brought in to organize a defensive strategy against the ruthless Nazi subs.

Soon, the precautions were in place, and Admiral Donitz ordered his U-boats south, where a new harvest of tonnage awaited. The New Jersey shore breathed a bit easier.

THE DAY THE BOARDWALK CAME FROM THE SEA

This is a volume dedicated to the shipwrecks off the coast of Ocean City and environs, true. This story, however, is not only of a wrecked seagoing vessel, but of a strange ironic twist that gave those who live on the land a certain element of revenge on the often stingy and vengeful sea.

It was May 1, 1948. Captain Harry Hubert of Atlantic City was heading out on his excursion boat, "Lone Ranger," when somebody spotted a life raft bobbing in the waves about five miles from shore.

Upon closer examination, it was discovered that the 25-passenger raft was empty, except for some life preservers and a logbook. Floating around the raft, though, were logs of a very different sort.

Capt. Hubert described the scene as "acres of pilings," and many 55-gallon drums. It was obvious that a barge laden with these items had foundered, and this motley flotsam was marking the spot.

Hubert headed back to port, and turned over the logbook to Coast Guard officials. They quickly put out a radio warning for all ships and boats to steer clear of the wreckage area. A call to the New York Coast Guard station revealed that the owners of the barge had reported its sinking, and all hands were saved.

The barge, the "Darien," out of Sand's Point, Maryland, was a 924-ton vessel which carried some 800 long pilings and Caterpillar tractor motors.

The sinking occurred in forty feet of water, and doubtlessly the tractor motors went right to the bottom.

Not so, however, for the pilings. As wood is wont to do, they floated. When Capt. Hubert initially reported the discovery to the "Lone Ranger's" owner, Capt. Clarence Starn, Capt. Starn said he'd expect the pilings to start washing up on shore near Ocean City or Longport before long.

Capt. Starn's prophecy began to be fulfilled already by the middle of the first week of May. This wreckage from the sea became the bounty for those on land, as state highway department workers were called in to begin rounding up the long logs that started rolling in the surf of Longport. The borough's bulldozer was used to haul the logs to the street ends of 14th, 16th and 24th Avenues, and the borough would lay claim to them and figure out what could be done to put them to good use.

These were massive pieces of valuable southern pine. They averaged two feet in diameter and eighty to ninety feet in length. All told, about a dozen of the pilings made their way to shore.

The gift from the surf couldn't have come at a better time for the embattled borough commissioners. Four years prior, most of Longport's boardwalk was wiped out by a storm. The former Coast Guard boathouse was dismantled and its lumber used for boardwalk underpinnings, and most of the former boardwalk was rebuilt, up to about 22nd Avenue. At that point, the borough simply ran out of money.

Residents between 22nd and 24th Avenues were disgruntled because their stretch of the wooden promenade was not restored. But the arrival of the pilings from the wreck came as good news for the residents and their commissioners, who immediately saw a golden opportunity.

If the lumber would have to have been purchased, it would have cost about $150 per thousand boardfeet. The logs from the wreck could be milled into suitable twelve and sixteen-feet lengths for about $20 per thousand boardfeet.

Within months, a new 12-feet wide boardwalk extended beyond 22nd Ave. in Longport—thanks to the wreck of the barge "Darien!"

THE SLOW DEATH OF THE ASTRA

When two ships collide, or when a storm overcomes a vessel at sea, Davy Jones usually has his way. But sometimes, the death of a ship at the relentless hands of the sea does not come without a struggle.

The collision of the Danish freighter "Astra" and Isthmian Line's "Steel Inventor" is a classic tale of a maritime mishap. The rain and fog of Friday, March 29, 1951 contributed to the collision, but the weight advantage of the Steel Inventor (5,698 tons to the Astra's 2,709) would be the deciding factor as the Danish vessel went down for the count in the sea a dozen miles off the Ocean City beaches.

The Astra was a coastal workhorse, this time bound for Havana, Cuba with cargo of general merchandise, foodstuffs and steel from the warehouses of New York City. Also aboard the Astra were more than 90 new automobiles that went down with the ship.

The Steel Inventor, which had just been involved in a collision with a pier the previous week, was northbound in the fog when it suddenly came upon the Astra and broadsided the lighter vessel, and split it in two.

There was no doubt from the outset that the Astra was dealt a deadly blow. The Steel Inventor's crew swarmed to the deck, at once checking damage on their own ship and looking for survivors on board the stricken Astra.

The larger vessel was damaged, but could easily weather the storm and make it to its appointed port. All of the Astra's crewmen were safely removed to the Steel Inventor.

In the meantime, rescue craft from the mainland were speeding to the scene, only to be rebuffed time and time again by the heavy seas and driving rains.

It wasn't until daybreak the next morning that outsiders could survey the damage. The bow of the Astra was poking out of the waves at a precarious angle, buoyed by a pocket of air that stubbornly refused to release the section of ship from its grasp.

The stern section of the Astra was already split away in the 85-feet deep water. William L. Mackey, a reporter for the Atlantic City Press-Union, provided readers with a stirring account of the scene:

> From 1000 feet in the air the shadowy outline of the midship and after portions of the Astra could be seen wallowing slowly from side to side beneath the sea's surface.
>
> Every few moments, the intense pressure of the sea brought crates and debris belching up from the bowels of the fully-loaded holds.
>
> Lumber and other buoyant objects which had gone adrift floated over a wide expanse of sea.
>
> Occasionally, a heavy sea rolling over the foundered freighter would force air into the holds and in its escape would cover the surface with huge, foaming bubbles.

Later, the pounding of the waves robbed the severed head of the Astra of its precious air and it joined its tail section on the sandy floor of the sea.

Still, the Astra somehow refused to disappear from sight without leaving something behind. Even after both sections of the hull had sunk, the forward and aft masts continued to rise above the surface.

Deemed a hazard to navigation, the masts were eventually removed.

Shards of the Astra's life continued to exist long after the death of the ship, as pieces of debris and the ship's cargo were reported on the ocean and beaches of Atlantic City and Ocean City for several days.

And, although the Astra is dead and gone, its memory is preserved in the minds of those who now dive on her remains, fish above those remains, and especially those who lived to tell their stories about that foggy day in March, 1951.

DIVERS' DELIGHTS

Fishermen and divers love shipwrecks. For them, these piles of steel, stone and scrap are havens for shellfish, game fish and adventure.

Oft times, however, little is known about the wreckage upon which these men and women ply their pastimes. The intent of this book has been to pull together from many sources information about the wrecks off the coast of Ocean City and environs. But even exhaustive research could not ascertain much information about several of the better-known dive and fish spots just off shore.

Many of the wrecks are that of barges, such as the John F.

McIlvaine, a 414-ton vessel built in 1903. The McIlvaine went down May 10, 1923 on the Great Egg Bar, and Coast Guard attempts to pull her from the sand failed.

This is all that's known about the barge, and that is typical of so many others.

The sea bottom is littered with anonymous wrecks and piles of debris, and little has been done to identify them. The result is a local name being applied to the wreckage for the purpose of identification.

The "Pig Iron Wreck" is one of these. Today identified only by the cargo it carried and took to the bottom, the Pig Iron Wreck is really that of the "Nay Aug," an 842-ton wooden barge out of New York's Durham Navigation Company.

One of 29 barges owned by Durham, the Nay Aug had a 35-foot beam and drew 15'3" of water. It was built in Connecticut in 1890 and sank in 1932 in the fish haven south of Ocean City.

While most of the wrecks with unexplained pasts have received unexplainable names, there are times that neither the ship's history nor the reason for the wreck site's monicker can be secured.

The seven-feet tall mound of wreckage called the "$25 Wreck" is an example. Why it is called what it is called is a mystery to even the veteran divers of the area. They know that it lies in 86 feet of water, and they know that large lobsters, as well as old bottles and brass spikes have been found on the wreck. They presume it was an old sailing ship or converted barge, but when asked about the origin of the "$25 Wreck" tag, they shake their heads.

The same is true for the "Southern Pet Wreck." It's fairly well accepted that this is the remains of the "Elizabeth Warren," a clam boat that sank in the late 1960s. Resting in 50 feet of water, the wreck stands about eight feet off the bottom. All that's left is the remnants of the wooden hull, and a large engine. Several years ago, Roger Fehrle of "East Coast Divers" managed to free the boat's 32-inch wheel from its mounting.

This, then, using the simplest criteria, should have become known as the "Wheel Wreck." That is, if one bases the logic on the next story.

The "Bell Wreck" is called by that name because a diver several years ago retrieved a large brass bell from the wreckage that sits in three pieces in 68 feet of water just outside the Avalon Shoal.

The hull is virtually disintegrated, although there is some wood planking under the sand. Visibility and bottom conditions are usually quite good.

The Bell Wreck is often mistakenly called the "Salem," but the wreckage of the Salem is actually a mile southeast of the Bell Wreck. Actually, the Bell Wreck is presumed to be a large and very old tug. The central piece of equipment in the wreckage is a massive engine, which appears to be upside down in the sand.

There is a bit of a different twist to the name, the "Stone Wreck." The name applies not to the vessel, the cargo, or to a particular underwater landmark of note. The "Stone Wreck" is so named because that's all that's down there. The presence of a pile of stones on the sand-mud bottom could very well indicate that they are all that remains of an ancient, probably 18th century, sailing ship.

With another underwater seamark dubbed the "Mud Wreck," it is believed that there is no wreck whatsoever in the 80-feet depths. The sea floor rises dramatically in the vicinity, just north-northeast of the Avalon Shoal, and the "wreck" is actually a bed of New Jersey coral. Divers know it as a prime area for lobsters, and call a part of the area "Honey Hole."

Another wreck that shows up on local charts is that called "Funny Face." This one is relatively simple to understand. The name of the wreck site was the name of a clam boat that went down with its edible cargo in 1981.

Totally inedible was the cargo of a pile of debris now called the "Oil Wreck." Hailed as a good dive site, the steel bones of this former American Oil Company barge protrude 10 feet up from the bottom in 60 feet of water.

The wreck caused a minor stir in 1984 when a storm caused a major stir underwater. An entire side of the squared-off system of framework was exposed by the storm's underwater action, and large brass hatches and other artifacts were suddenly revealed to divers who ventured to the wreck.

PLANNED SHIPWRECKS

There is no doubt whatsoever that ships will continue to wreck along the New Jersey coastline. All the intricate electronic gadgetry and pinpoint weather forecasting of the late 20th century will not prevent nature and misfortune from reaping their toll.

Similarly, man has chosen to give nature a boost from time to time by building artificial reefs, many times with the useless old hulks of ships.

It would be ludicrous to call these planned events "shipwrecks," but as time passes, the presence of sunken vessels in fairly shallow waters will be questioned by novice divers and fishermen who discover them.

The most recent addition to a growing series of "fish havens" in the sport fishing banks from Barnegat to Corson's Inlets is the "Morania Abaco."

This 1500-ton former asphalt carrier was built in Camden, New Jersey, in 1958, and served its masters well during its lifetime. It was one of many anonymous steamers that plied the northeastern coasts, and probably was destined for a trip to the scrap yard upon retirement.

Instead, the 265-feet long ship, stripped of anything useful and devoid of any protruding item that could become hazardous to navigation, was towed from its berth in Staten Island to a point about 12 miles off Great Egg Harbor Inlet.

Ironically, the rough seas that more often prove to be the undoing of a ship at sea, proved to give the Morania Abaco a stay of execution several times.

Several times the death squads attempted to tow the condemned tanker to sea, and several times the sea said no.

Finally, the old ship, donated for such a purpose by the oil company that owned it, was tugged to the appointed spot and rigged with plastic explosives.

In a shattering burst of smoke, light and sound, the Morania Abaco was given enough damage to sink her, while still preserving most of the hull for its second use.

On the bottom, the ship's carcass will slowly act as a magnet for marine life. Three other ships that met similar fates rest nearby, and collectively they will attract small organisms that will be eaten by larger ones that will be . . . that will become a food chain.

The artificial reef program is a project of the Marine Fisheries Administration of New Jersey, with the cooperation and financial support of private concerns. The Morania Abaco was towed and sunken with the help of a grant from "The Fishermen" magazine.

Thus, the readers of that magazine will find a new and fertile fishing ground when the underwater food chain matures. The Morania Abaco and the three other ships, the "Pauline Marie," "First Lady" and the "America," will live on to serve their masters again.

ACKNOWLEDGEMENTS

The authors would like to thank those individuals and organizations who have provided guidance, assistance, resources, time and inspiration during the research and compilation of this volume.

This is always an agonizing chore for researchers and writers, seeking to mention all who were instrumental in the effort. It is with this in mind that the following are recognized. Any oversights are deeply regretted.

Much thanks to the Ocean City Historical Museum, Ocean City, N.J.; United States Coast Guard Station, Ocean City (Petty Officer Michael Rauch); Senior Studio, Ocean City; East Coast Dive Supply, Northfield, N.J. (Roger Fehrle, dive instructor); Atlantic County Library, Atlantic City, N.J.; Cape May County Library, Cape May Court House, N.J.; Philadelphia Maritime Museum, Philadelphia, Pa. (Kay Dwain, librarian); Reading Public Library, Reading, Pa.; Albright College Library, Reading, Pa.; Reading Eagle-Times, Reading, Pa.; Steamship Historical Society of America, New York, N.Y.; University of Baltimore Library, Baltimore, Md. (Laura F. Brown, Steamship Historical Society of America Collections librarian); Hon. Gus Yatron, Pennsylvania 6th District Congressman (Elwood Broad, staff assistant); Library of Congress, Washington, D.C. (John A. Wolter, chief); United States Coast Guard Arts and Artifacts, Washington, D.C.; National Archives, Still Pictures Branch, Washington, D.C.; Naval Historical Center, Ship Survey Branch, Washington, D.C. (John Reilly).

Without the help of these and others, this book would still be just a dream in the mind of its authors

ABOUT THE AUTHORS

David J. Seibold, of Wyomissing Hills, Pa. and Barnegat Light, N.J., is an avid boater, fisherman and diver. He is a former commodore of the Rajah Temple (Shrine) Yacht Club of Reading, Pa., and is a member of the Reading and Barnegat Light Scuba and Rescue Teams.

Seibold is a graduate of Pennsylvania State University and served as a company commander in the Viet Nam campaign after being commissioned in the U.S. Army Signal Corps.

An active Rotarian and member of several other civic and social organizations, Seibold is employed as an account executive at radio station WEEU in Reading, Pa.

Charles J. Adams III is also employed at WEEU radio, as Public Affairs Director. He also is a travel and entertainment writer for the Reading Eagle newspaper. A. U.S Navy veteran, Adams serves on the board of directors of the Pennsylvania State University Alumni Society of the Berks Campus and is a school director in the Exeter Township (Pa.) School District.

Adams is also vice-president of the Board of Trustees of the Reading Public Library and serves on the executive council and editorial board of the Historical Society of Berks County.

OTHER BOOKS BY CHARLES J. ADAMS III AND DAVID J. SEIBOLD

"Ghost Stories of Berks County" (Adams, 1983)
"Ghost Stories of Berks County, Book Two" (Adams, 1984)
"Shipwrecks Near Barnegat Inlet" (Seibold & Adams, 1984)
"Legends of Long Beach Island" (Seibold & Adams, 1985)

SHIPWRECKS OFF OCEAN CITY

by DAVID J. SEIBOLD
and CHARLES J. ADAMS III

Drama on the high sea from Absecon to Avalon

PHOTO GALLERY

The four-masted bark "Sindia," seen shortly after it beached near 17th Street in Ocean City in December, 1901. (Photo courtesy of Senior Studio and the Ocean City Historical Museum)

The tide and sand have taken their toll on the wreck of the iron-hulled "Sindia" in this photo, taken in the early 1900s. (Courtesy of Senior Studio and the Ocean City Historical Museum)

This is said to be the figurehead of the "Sindia," and is on display at the Ocean City Historical Museum. (Photo by Charles J. Adams III)

The "Sindia" became a curiosity after it washed ashore on the 17th Street beach on December 15, 1901. (Photo courtesy of Senior Studio and the Ocean City Historical Museum)

Examples of the "Sindia's" cargo are on display at the Ocean City Historical Museum. The name board in the foreground features letters taken from the ship's bow. (Photo by Charles J. Adams III)

A lone horseman surveys the stark remains of the "Sindia" several years after her stranding. (Photo courtesy of Senior Studio and the Ocean City Historical Museum)

An old post card depicts the "Sindia" beginning to break up in the Ocean City surf.

Members of a Life-saving Service crew are depicted in an old post card.

The "Texel" was one of several ships exploded by a German submarine off the coast on June 2, 1918. (Photo courtesy of the Steamship Historical Society of America)

THE RECONSTRUCTED CAROLINA

Another victim of the June 2, 1918 raids by German subs on east coast shipping was the "Carolina." (Courtesy of the Steamship Historical Society of America)

More than 50 members of this ship, the "Cayru," died when the vessel was torpedoed by a Nazi submarine on March 8, 1942. (Photo courtesy of the Steamship Historical Society of America)

Bound from Buenos Aires to New York, the "Rio Tercero" sank off the coast of Ocean City on June 22, 1942. (Courtesy of the Steamship Historical Society of America)

The freighter, "Lemuel Burrows," was sunk in March, 1942, while off the coast of Ocean City. She is seen here coming through the Panama Canal in 1928. (Courtesy of the Steamship Historical Society of America)

The "San Jose" went down after colliding with the "Santa Eliza" on January 17, 1942. The "San Jose," seen above, was a 3,358-ton ship owned by the United Fruit Company. (Courtesy of the Steamship Historical Society of America)

The "Almirante," seen above, now lies in ruins beneath the sea, and is known by Ocean City divers and fishermen as the "Flour Wreck." (Photo courtesy of the Steamship Historical Society of America)

The "City of Athens," which sank after a collision with the French navy cruiser "La Glorie" on May 1, 1918. (Courtesy of the Steamship Historical Society of America)

This gun, mounted on the freighter, "Varanger," failed to prevent the ship from being sunk by a Nazi submarine torpedo in 1942. (Courtesy of the Steamship Historical Society of America)

The cannon in the foreground of this old post card picture was said to have come from the brig, "Delight," which wrecked at Ocean City in the late 18th century. The 9-pounder disappeared in 1964.

The prop of the sunken offshore clamming boat "Elizabeth Warner" (also known as the "Southern Pet Wreck") is displayed by (l. to r.) divers Roger Fehrle, Paul Callahan and Mike Weatherford. (Photo courtesy of East Coast Dive Supply)

ON THE BACK COVER: Sunlight highlights the stark remains of the ship, "Sindia," on the 17th Street beach in Ocean City. This tiller protruding out of the sand, as well as an occasional glimpse of other parts of the hull, are all that remain visible of the ship that ran aground in 1901. (Photo by Charles J. Adams III)